ENVIRONMENTAL DESIGN

The Best of Architecture & Technology

Margaret Cottom-Winslow

The Library of Applied Design

An Imprint of **PBC INTERNATIONAL**, Inc.

Distributor to the book trade in the United States and Canada:

Rizzoli International Publications Inc.
300 Park Avenue South
New York, NY 10010

Distributor to the art trade in the United States:

Letraset USA
40 Eisenhower Drive
Paramus, NJ 07652

Distributor to the art trade in Canada:

Letraset Canada Limited
555 Alden Road
Markham, Ontario L3R 3L5, Canada

Distributed throughout the rest of the world:

Hearst Books International
105 Madison Avenue
New York, NY 10016

Library of Congress Cataloging-in-Publication Data
Cottom-Winslow, Margaret.
    Environmental design: the best of architecture and
technology / by Margaret Cottom-Winslow.
            p.   cm.
    Includes index.
    ISBN 0-86636-123-5
    1. Architecture—Environmental aspects.   2. Architecture—
Human factors.   3. Architecture, Modern—20th century.
I. Title.
NA2542.35.C68   1990   90-13201
720'.47—dc20   CIP

*CAVEAT—Information in this text is believed accurate, and
will pose no problem for the student or casual reader.
However, the authors were often constrained by information
contained in signed release forms, information that could
have been in error or not included at all. Any
misinformation (or lack of information) is the result of failure
in these attestations. The author has done whatever is
possible to insure accuracy.*

For information about our audio products, write us at:
Newbridge Book Clubs, 3000 Cindel Drive, Delran, NJ 08370

Color separation, printing and binding by
Toppan Printing Co. (H.K.) Ltd. Hong Kong

Typography by
Jeanne Weinberg Typesetting

10 9 8 7 6 5 4 3 2 1

CONTENTS

To Harold Stump.   *Teacher.*   *Critic.*   *Friend.*

PROLOGUE

Hopes and Regrets

"*Here is summarized the program of the planning of a city, in which it is exemplified that work is the human law and that there is enough of the ideal in the cult of beauty and order to endow life with splendor.*"

Dora Wiebenson
Tony Garnier—THE CITE INDUSTRIELLE
GEORGE BRAZILLER, NEW YORK: 1969

"*Modern architecture is a product of Western civilization. It began to take shape during the later eighteenth century, with the democratic and industrial revolutions that formed the modern age. Like all architecture, it has attempted to create a special environment for human life and to image the thoughts and actions of human beings as they have wished to believe themselves to be. In these two fundamental attempts the modern man has faced psychic difficulties unparalleled in the West since the time of the breakup of Rome.*"

Vincent Scully, Jr.—*MODERN ARCHITECTURE,*
GEORGE BRAZILLER, NEW YORK: 1967

FOREWORD

GROWING UP IN THE SAN JOAQUIN VALLEY IN California I was surrounded by both the earth's largesse and man's creative genius—fields of wildflowers, majestic mountain ranges, oil refineries, railroads, jet propulsion. The combination of the natural and the technological didn't appear to be dichotomous until the wildflowers began to disappear and sand storms blotted out the sun. Today smog nestles into the cleft of the Sierra Nevadas and the Coast Range. The jet planes and the refineries contribute to this malevolent miasma and those majestic snow capped peaks are no longer visible.

Watching this erosion of the natural landscape is still a painful memory. What person who has waded knee keep through fields of lupin and poppies would not wait each Spring for the miracle to reoccur? But the fragile interrelationship of man and nature was fixed in my mind when each year there were fewer and fewer flowers and more houses and roads. Nothing the earth has to offer can be taken for granted and beauty must be cherished in order to be sustained.

This education of what the earth offers to man and what man owes to the earth was continued and reinforced by the faculty of The College of Architecture at the University of California at Berkeley. There we argued the architect's responsibilities to the client, and to the environment. The synthesis of technology and natural landscape in the works of Bernard Maybeck,

Frank Lloyd Wright, and Bruce Goff as opposed to the technological approach of Mies van der Rohe were serious points of discussion. I've no doubt that these early lessons have influenced every path I've taken and every creative effort I've attempted. In many ways, this book is a distillation of those thoughts and lessons learned from the earth and from many creative minds. I'm grateful for this teaching.

I'm also grateful to my sons, Curt and Brad for their years of support and encouragement. In their own way they espouse the principles I've alluded to. And to my "midwives"—my classmate, colleague and friend, Barney Jensen who can distill complex ideas into coherent thoughts, my editor Kevin Clark who wields a firm and gentle hand, and my agent Richard Barber who with grace and intelligence lent his support and encouragement—thank you. Your humor and mutual dedication to the environment has sustained me.

I hope this book also offers sustenance to those architects and designers who offered their work to illustrate these ideas. The creative minds who conceived and built these structures are the minds who possess the capacity to nurture and revitalize this wonderful planet. We all use technology and technology offers so much that's good and productive. All of us need to understand, however, that balance and restraint are called for at this time in our evolution. We must control technology and use it carefully and judiciously. The earth will bless us.

M.C-W.
April 22, 1990
Earth Day

THE EFFECTS OF INVENTIONS—*The Good and The Bad*

The inventions triggered by the discoveries of the "Industrial Revolution" have revolutionized our lives. We no longer travel in cold, uncomfortable coaches, victimized by weather and the limits of tired animals stretched to their endurance. We no longer huddle next to a smoking fireplace on cold, blustery nights while the wind howls into the cracks and crevices of stone or log houses. We no longer die of pneumonia, or infantile paralysis, or syphilis; sanitation and sewage systems have added to our health and comfort, and concrete paving has saved a lot of shoes and hems and trousers from incrustations of mud.

Consider how the Industrial Revolution has altered our concept of time. How long did it take to travel to even a distant town before the steam engine, the automobile, the airplane or the rocket? Hours, days, weeks, months, years. Now we measure global travel in hours. Space travel might be measured in months, even years—to reach the farthest galaxies, and when reports from the space probes are sent back to Earth, our perceptions of the world could be altered irrevocably. If you think about it, in many ways we're victims of the Chinese curse, "May you live in interesting times!" This last quarter of the twentieth century is certainly interesting technologically—and even politically. The advent of the "Age of Communication" has brought about political upheavals, medical and scientific breakthroughs—and global pollution on a scale unimagined even fifty years ago.

Many critics, scientists and philosophers feel that this is the price mankind must pay for worshiping and being slaves to technology and "progress." There are those who want to return to the "Craft Age" and "Basic Values." The "machine" is seen as a Godless icon and technology as the curse of mankind. But, let's examine this philosophy—this potential thrust of civilization, at least in terms of building and shaping the environment.

ALTERING THE LANDSCAPE—*The Fine Touch of The Hand of Man*

Look around. There are very few places in the landscape today where the hand of man is not visible. Granted, some of these "human touches" leave much to be desired and have desecrated the landscape. No one denies that, and certainly this book does not seek to justify and excuse the rape of the landscape for profit, greed or thoughtlessness. Just the opposite. This book hopes to show the good that man has done in altering the landscape through technology. How technology has (along with the undeniable destructive imprint) improved not only our health and saved us time, but has contributed to our psychological well being by allowing talented members of the design community—worldwide—to create environments that enhance our lives and psyches.

To further explore the effects of technology upon man's need to alter his environment, let's go back and also examine the interaction of man and technology. In fact, let's explore the two different definitions of technology from THE AMERICAN HERITAGE DICTIONARY OF THE ENGLISH LANGUAGE; Houghton Mifflin Company, 1976:

> "2. *Anthropology.* Broadly, the body of knowledge available to a civilization that is of use in fashioning implements, practicing manual arts and skills, and extracting or collecting materials."

> "1. *a.* The application of science, especially to industrial or commercial objectives. *b.* The entire body of methods and materials used to achieve those objectives."

By listing the two different definitions in reverse order, I'd like to make a point. The "Craft Age" that some would like to return to was also a "technological age." Different in degree and materials, perhaps, but technological, nonetheless. By his very nature, man seeks to alter and improve his surroundings—to find newer and better ways of accomplishing the same things.

That man has done this since the beginning of time becomes evident when you explore one of the caves in Les Eyzies in the Dordogne—Font de Gaume. We all know that cavemen decorated the walls of their habitations with incredible engravings and paintings. But, what's fascinating is that at Font de Gaume, the inhabitants of this prehistoric shelter also *altered* their dwelling place. Openings were carved for lookouts and niches for timbers were created to allow more than one level in the high vaulted interior of this cave. These are certainly crude forms of technology.

Once you admit to man's technological inventiveness, where does it stop? How much is enough? Who's to say what is "good" and what is "bad?" I'd like to think that there really is no "bad" technology, only inhumane uses of technology and its products. This, however, may be a naive approach. Certainly there's widespread pollution on the planet that comes out of the uses of technology.

THE EVIL FLOWERING OF INVENTION

The smog we breathe, the polluted water we drink, the acid rain that showers down on us, the garbage we can't dispose of—all these might be classed as the "evil flowers" of technology and the Industrial Revolution. No one disputes that these side effects have diminished the positive results of technological advances. Steel mills and chemical factories spew pollution into the air and water. Trains, automobiles, planes and rockets, leave behind toxic emissions that destroy lungs and lives. Industrial emissions blacken the air and the surrounding buildings. Refineries spoil the ground, the air and the visual landscape. There are those who feel that nuclear power warms our streams and oceans, alters the balance of nature and potentially threatens our unborn. We have our Love Canals and our toxic waste dumps. No one denies any of this.

But on balance, there are positive effects of invention. At the same time that the steel industry pollutes the air, it also creates materials with which to build low-cost housing. The chemical industries pollute the streams and, at the same time, provide plastics for synthetic materials that seal buildings and prevent heat loss. Reinforced concrete and steel allow vertical structures and, thus, produce more open space and preserve the natural landscape. Perhaps, at the present time, we have a trade-off.

Technology, since the Industrial Revolution, has given us innovative materials. Unfortunately, our production of these materials (and sometimes our use of them) has given us pollution and, in some ways, lessened our ability to live wholesome, sane, healthy lives. Yet, technology has also allowed us to experience worlds, peoples, and events that would be lost to us otherwise. And the built environment? Would you truly want a landscape with nothing but cabins, huts and caves? Doesn't man truly want to experience the grand, the unexpected, the glorious, the magnificent? Don't we want to be transcended, not just by nature, but by what we can create from nature and our own inventiveness and imagination—our "technology?" The historical facts seem to point this way.

MILESTONES OF THE PAST

Palace of Shapur I	**Daigoji Pagoda**
Persepolis	**Peking Palace; The Grand**
Babylon	**Ancestral Shrine**
Ziggurat of Dur-Untash	**Temple of Quetzalcoatl**
Pyramids at Giza	**Inca Citadel**
Mesa Verde	**Notre-Dame-La-Grande,**
Stonehenge	**Poitier**
Pont Du Gard	**Baptistery, Florence**
Maison Carree	**Chartres**
Pantheon	**Notre Dame**
Acropolis	**Salisbury Cathedral**
Angkor Vat	**St. Peters**
Taj Mahal	**Uffizi Palace**
Hagia Sophia	**Villa Rotunda**
Piazza San Marco	**Zimbabwe**
St. Basil	**The Brandenburg Gate**
Himeji Castle	**Monticello**

This list includes many of the architectural treasures of the world. All were built before the Industrial Revolution, and all made use of some form of innovative technology. And—I would venture to guess—that over the ages all these magnificent structures have, in some way, allowed man to experience the grand, the unexpected, the glorious and the magnificent. These monuments have allowed man to transcend nature and prove to himself that with his inventiveness and imagination he does not have to be at the mercy of the elements and the chance happenings of the natural environment. Perhaps, that's one of the reasons why man builds, not simply for shelter, but to prove he has some control over his life.

THE TOOLS OF OUR FUTURE

wood
concrete
steel
brick
glass
aluminum
bronze
copper
synthetics
masonry
ceramics
plastic laminates
fiberglass
adobe/earth

These materials are some of the resources every designer uses to create new and innovative design solutions. Whether the designer uses wood frame, post & lintel, domes, arches, lift slabs, concrete shells, geodesic domes, composite structures, flat plate and slab floor or post tensioned concrete construction, pre-cast concrete, tilt-up slabs, curtain walls, earth shelter construction, active or passive solar construction, prefabrication or air structures, the designer uses some form of technology. It may have its roots in the medieval world or the twentieth century. But, building by its very nature is technology, and the more the designer is conversant with the current technology, the more he or she is likely to come up with a new and better solution to the problem of altering the environment for the best uses of mankind.

One must be aware, however, that altering the environment is obvious. Architecture is obvious. Landscape design is obvious. A painter, a musician, a poet—perhaps even a scientist—can easily destroy what's faulty or unpleasing. Destroying architecture is more difficult. Not impossible, but obvious. Perhaps that's why, in some ways, architects might be more responsible to the needs of the environment and the destructive effects of technology. Their mistakes stand out.

The purpose of this book, however, is not to point out mistakes. The purpose is to show successes, how individuals have approached design problems through the best uses of technology and imagination, and how our lives have been improved because the created environments are soothing, esthetic, climatized, and they allow us to live and do our work in a realm conducive to human interaction. To this end, we'll explore environments in these categories:

Single Family Housing
Multiple Dwellings
Stadiums, Swimming Pools & Sports Complexes
Theaters & Concert Halls
Zoos, Aquariums & Historical Parks
Schools
Universities
Libraries
Museums
Seats of Government
Religious Buildings
Health Care Facilities
Office Spaces
Mixed-Use Buildings
Retail Stores & Shopping Malls
Hotels, Convention Centers & Study Centers
Financial Institutions
Factories & Industrial Buildings
Airports, Train, Subway & Bus Terminals
Parking Garages
Nuclear Installations

Keep in mind that each example in each category has an approach that adds to the human scale of the environment, and provides some element that enhances the landscape and/or the lives of people.

NEW WAYS OF THINKING

Another aim of this book is to explore ways in which technology has influenced the thinking of the designers whose work is illustrated. For example, *Paolo Soleri* began his work on ARCOSANTI in 1969. He states, "The concept is that of a structure called an *arcology,* or *ecological architecture.*" But could he, or would he, have envisioned cities of towers to preserve open spaces without the Industrial Revolution and the destruction of the natural environment that misuse of technology brought about? Some of the negative aspects of the Industrial Revolution—

pollution and urban blight—have inspired visionary and creative thinkers to develop new and revolutionary ideas.

The conceptual schemes for arcology settlements range from complexes floating in the ocean, complexes conceived as living bridges connecting two rims of a canyon, complexes of two mated pyramids rising 3500 feet into the air and covering half a square mile, to a space station— the *Asteromo*—a space city of 70,000 people designed to explore the stars.

Arcosanti—Paolo Soleri's realistic (and partially constructed) concept—vertical living in a complex of a single three-dimensional structure of concrete, glass and steel, tilted toward the sun—is a fascinating one. But, support for it has not been as forthcoming as he'd hoped. Today, actualization of his dream, completed buildings, are few. There are some concrete vaults, some cubic structures and an amphitheater. However, he continues to pursue his dream of integrating the technological world into the natural landscape so the best of both are utilized.

Technology is also necessary if we're to preserve not only the landscape, but our global architectural heritage. The STATUE OF LIBERTY, for example, underwent a complete restoration in 1986. The architects of *Swanke Hayden Connell Architects* and *The Office of Thierry W. Despont* found a number of ways in which technology not only allowed them to complete their task, but to improve the accessibility of this landmark. The new interior elevator, for example, might not have been possible except for the use of laser technology to survey the interior space.

Replacing the interior iron armature that connects the skin to the framework was another major problem; it was badly rusted and decayed. This condition led the architects to look for a replacement material other than iron that would not be subjected to the same conditions. They chose stainless steel 316L for the armature bars, and ferallium (a high-strength alloy of steel and aluminum with a springlike quality) for the flat bars. Neither material was available when the statue was erected.

In terms of other technologies used on the restoration, it's important to note that x-ray analysis was used to search for hidden cracks in the structure. Computer photogrammetry was used to model the new flame and working with General Electric, two different colored metal halide lamps were developed to light the torch.

In the final analysis, the designers' task was, of course, restoration—to preserve and restore what sculptor Frederic-Auguste Bartholdi and engineer Alexandre-Gustave Eiffel visualized and actualized. In this they succeeded. They also succeeded in satisfying their own needs to create something lasting and of incomparable impact. In their book, *Restoring the Statue of Liberty*, McGraw-Hill Book Company, 1986, which describes this restoration process, Richard Seth Hayden and Thierry Despont describe it this way,

"We have restored the statue's health without
tampering with her dignity."

Dignity is a vital component not only of a work of art but of the human condition.

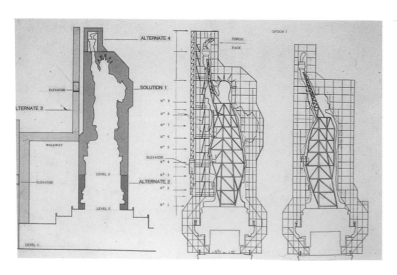

ACCESSIBILITY & UPGRADING

In the restoration of the Statue of Liberty, the architects were able to install an emergency elevator and perhaps make the statue handicapped-accessible. In the upgrading and restoration of the PARTHENON in Nashville, Tennessee, the architects of *Gresham, Smith and Partners* sought to provide a new entrance to the museum, improve the exhibit spaces, provide support areas—and make it handicapped-accessible. In this case they succeeded by going underground and using an existing interior wythe of a wall built along the inside face of the east and west facades.

This elevator and the use of a ramp network has opened this otherwise inaccessible historic replica to use by the handicapped. It's interesting to contemplate how many areas and structures which are now inaccessible could be altered through ramps, elevators, stair lifts and the like.

In terms of altering the historic exterior of the building, the new construction had minimum visual impact, while providing the much needed storage and support spaces. The interior gallery spaces have been described as "sober and subdued, dignified yet quietly dramatic." All the things good gallery space should be.

It's also interesting to note that the reviewer, Trond Sandvick for *Art Commentary*, used the word "dignified," as did Richard Hayden and Thierry Despont. Perhaps "dignified" is a word to contemplate. Human beings should always be allowed to retain their dignity. Thus, the case for the handicapped. Being barred from a structure because there's no way for a wheelchair to enter cannot be a dignified circumstance. What about the use of materials?

Surely the original Parthenon would be described as dignified—through its use of materials and its form. And the same can be said for this replica. So perhaps dignity is a quality we should assess when we choose and discard materials and seek to build with new technological materials and techniques.

A FINAL NOTE—*The Benefits Reaped*

As you read the following pages and gaze in wonder and admiration at the work these architects and designers have produced during the past fifteen years, try to keep in mind the aspects of our lives that have been improved by technology, ways in which technology has allowed us to keep or improve our sense of human dignity. If you stop to consider it, the ways in which we live and work can either enhance our dignity or rob us of it. Consider the workplace. Is it dignified to work in dark, hot, cramped spaces? Is it dignified to live in cold, damp, airless cells? Can one have dignity and self worth if there are no open spaces, no green areas, no glimpses of the sky?

Technology has allowed the average man a better existence in many ways. In the buildings we design and construct today we can incorporate *space, light, sound-proofing, central heating, air conditioning, automation, open space* and *indoor garden areas*. Each one of these attributes contributes to our health and well being.

EXAMPLES, IDEAS & GENIUS

On the following pages you'll find over a hundred architectural examples from many parts of the world—all using technology in some way to actualize the ideas of the client or the architect—or both. A building is, after all, the result of a partnership between the architect and the client. And it's the architect's task to interpret the client's dream—his vision—infuse it with his own genius and vision, and give it form. The form comes out of the way in which he visualizes and captures the spaces and fills them with light.

The samples showcased here are from a diverse range. Some are huge complexes, some are small and modest. The selection is deliberate. To show the range of technology, it's important to show how it affects building forms from the modest to the grand, from the economical to the luxurious, some show genius and some show craftsmanship. But, they all show how the Industrial Revolution has altered everyone's life.

RESIDENTIAL ARCHITECTURE

‘‘One can imagine a city of tomorrow in which the residential buildings (once the extreme, arrogant ostentation of the aristocratic palace of the past or the pitiable pretentiousness of most of the buildings of today has been abandoned) will assume a limpid, clear and honest constructional sincerity, made lively and gay by well studied relationships between streets, plazas and gardens.’’

PIER LUIGI NERVI
‘‘Is Architecture Moving Toward Unchangeable Forms?’’
Structure in Art and in Science

Housing, both single family and multiple dwellings existed before the Industrial Revolution, and in many areas of the world, the shape and configuration of the housing units does appear to be much different today than it was in the 1800s. Yet, while the appearance may be the same, the quality of the environment within the housing units themselves is quite different.

The environmental aspects (light, space, air quality, heating, ventilation, sanitation) that contribute to quality of life have been vastly improved by the Industrial Revolution, both by the nature of building materials themselves, and by new and innovative building techniques. Light and space are two of the qualities, for example that have been improved by better materials and techniques. Large panes of glass and materials that can span large distances— these are only two aspects of what technology has contributed to the improved quality of the housing of today.

Possibly, one can break up residential architecture into two main categories: single family housing and multiple dwellings. Each category of housing has its own restrictions and advantages.

■ MULTIPLE DWELLINGS

Multiple dwellings create a different set of problems. In these building forms the challenge is to create multiple, attached spaces within which a client can actualize his dreams.

There is some concern that overpopulation and scarcity of land have created the need for multiple dwelling units. However, if one takes a more historical view, it appears that many other factors have influenced the development of apartment houses, housing complexes, and new towns. The phenomenon of multiple housing has both an anthropological basis and a technological basis.

From the beginnings of man's history, dwellings were communal and, one might say, multiple. The members of a tribe or clan lived together in caves, cliff dwellings, or nomadic communities. Granted, there were individual areas for social units, but the concept was that of housing the entire cohesive entity together for safety from enemies, convenience in food gathering and growing, and continuity in passing along values and traditions. This is a very old concept and one which, although not altogether used in the same context, fits into the uses of technology.

For example, steel and the elevator might be seen as the ''fathers'' of the apartment house—of the concept of multiple dwellings. This concept had some of its contemporary beginnings in Chicago after the fire of 1871.

After the fire, the need for housing was so acute that Chicago architects conceived of the apartment house as the solution to their immediate problem. Apartment houses are suited to the urban lifestyle, and many cities have adopted this as an intelligent solution to the problem of housing masses of people within a limited area. But, the concept of the apartment house might not have been actualized without the genius of William LeBaron Jenney (who had been trained as an engineer) nor without the technological materials to achieve his innovative vision—''skeleton construction.''

No matter what type of housing an individual or family chooses to live in, there are still certain qualities that contribute to a livable environment. On the following pages

are some examples of what are livable and innovative environments in different climates and different countries, and all have benefitted from technology and the innovative ideas of the designers.

■ SINGLE FAMILY HOUSING

Technology has created fewer changes in the single family dwelling than in any other building form, except in the field of energy conservation. One might argue the depletion of fossil fuels, and squandering of energy since the Industrial Revolution is responsible for this, but that's not entirely true. Before the Industrial Revolution, coal was used as fuel in Britain because most of the forests were depleted, and in primitive societies today, forests have been depleted by using wood for warmth and cooking.

Primitive man began the depletion of resources. There was no conservation as we know it today, no reforestation or crop rotation; experts are debating whether the civilizations that vanished (long before the Industrial Revolution) did so because of drought, natural disasters or the like. Events that perhaps could have been alleviated by technology.

Technology can begin to alter the balance between what resources man has at his disposal and how he can effectively use those resources for a continuing, comfortable life. For example, technology has been responsible for the understanding and use of solar power as an energy alternative. With that in mind, we'll look at some examples of homes in different climates that depend on solar power.

At the same time we'll also look at some single family residences that have been designed with beauty, function, and advantageous use of the site. In our private homes, as nowhere else, we can use materials to express our deepest desires. When an architect designs for a private client, he can indulge that client's secret desires for a nurturing environment. As long, of course, as he stays within the client's budget. Perhaps, here is where technology can be used most effectively: by using innovative materials and techniques that have come about since the Industrial Revolution, a designer can sometimes make a client's dreams reality.

PROJECT NAME:
Desert Retreat
LOCATION:
Phoenix, Arizona
ARCHITECT:
The Leonard Parker Associates: Leonard S. Parker, principal-in-charge; Mark Pearson, project manager; Ray Greco, project architect; in association with: The Alliance Southwest
PHOTOGRAPHY:
A.F. Payne

Desert Retreat

Phoenix, Arizona

Preserving the Integrity of the Desert

The charge of the owners of this DESERT RETREAT, was that the completed structure fit "unobtrusively and comfortably" into the desert landscape. At the same time, they wanted to take advantage of the view. There was, however, one obstacle. The City Hillside Ordinance prohibited disturbing the

major wash that runs diagonally through the site. The architects—The Leonard Parker Associates with The Alliance Southwest—solved this problem by bridging over the wash and leaving this part of the site untouhced.

The use of natural materials that required little or no maintenance was another client stipulation. The house was also to be energy efficient. To satisfy the client's requirements, the architects used indigenous desert stone, stucco and glass to accomplish the first priority, and passive and active solar systems to accomplish the second. Deep overhangs and automatically activated solar screens to shade the south wall were part of the solar components of the design. In the interior, the architects used clerestories to provide natural lighting without direct solar gain.

Marble floors and vaulted ceilings of hardwood were used as natural materials for the interior. These, in combination with the siting of the structure, create a residence that is at home in its surroundings. In this example of a successful integration of a building form with the landscape, one sees the influence of the cliff dwellers of the Arizona desert in both form and materials. A sheltering interior environment has been created that protects the inhabitants from the harsh desert environment.

Island House

Mattapoisett, Massachusetts

PROJECT NAME:
Island House
LOCATION:
Mattapoisett, Massachusetts
CLIENT:
Robert Frank
ARCHITECT:
CBT/Childs Bertman Tseckares & Casendino Inc.:
Richard Bertman FAIA, principal; Doug Fisher, job
captain
PHOTOGRAPHY:
Nick Wheeler
AWARD:
Excellence in Design, 1987—Red Cedar Shingle
Handsplit Shake Bureau

*An Off-Shore Island
Dwelling*

When asked if this building could have been completed before the Industrial Revolution, the architects replied, ''a house such as this, conceived to maximize views, take advantage of wind and sun angles, and minimize energy usage by design would have been conceived before the Industrial Revolution.'' Well put.

The cruciform plan developed by

CBT/Childs, Bertman Tseckares & Casendino

Inc. for the Island House radiates from a

central mechanical core, thus allowing

maximum views from all sides. The high

central space of what almost appears to be a

pyramidal concept forms a natural

ventilation core, and the orientation protects

areas from the southwesterly winds.

The ambiance of the house reflects the best of the seaside resort architecture of the area, and some views evoke memories of early lighthouses. The architectural tradition is clearly eastern in concept and the wood frame construction, while not a product of industrialization, nevertheless, is used in such a way to create an environment that takes full advantage of the climate and the site.

The site and the views from the four sides of the cruciform plan were what inspired the design of this house. It sits on its lonely and windswept site as a beacon of the elegance of efficient design.

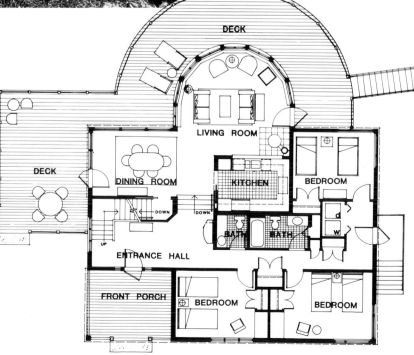

PROJECT NAME:
Ludgin House
LOCATION:
Georgetown Island, Maine
CLIENT:
Don and Sue Ludgin
ARCHITECT:
Hockamock Design with Nomad Builders:
Elisabeth King, architect; Leslie Hoffman, builder;
Norman Saunders, engineer
PHOTOGRAPHY:
Sue C. Ludgin (prints) and Elisabeth S. King (slides)

The Ludgin House

Georgetown Island, Maine

*Taking Advantage of
the Sun*

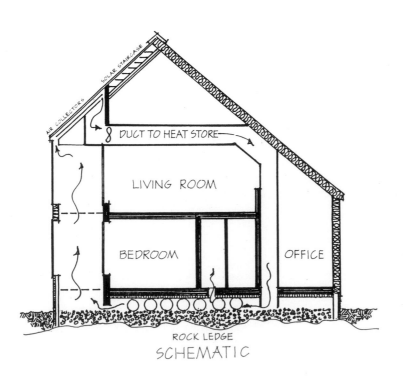

the LUDGIN HOUSE on Georgetown Island in Maine uses 100 percent solar heating. When the owners hired the architect, Elizabeth King, and the builders, Leslie Hoffman and Jaspen Towle they stipulated that the "solar staircase," invented by architect Norman Saunders should be part of the overall design. The "solar staircase," this unique configuration, is essentially a stepped pattern of mirrors in a unit assembly. The mirrors are set below a skylight at approximately a 12 degree pitch.

From the outside, it appears to be skylight, but on the inside this unit becomes an opaque glass ceiling that almost creates the effect of a rainbow. The owners need no artificial light before sunset and the entire structure is ventilated with fresh air through the two-story sun space. The house

also contains no furnace. The air from the collectors is ducted into the hypocaust that uses sixty 55-gallon drums of water as a thermal mall. All this is accomplished by using one fan. Although the living room does have a wood stove for additional heating, the use has been minimal.

The exterior of this solar structure is traditional in appearance. It speaks of the tradition and stability that's part of New England. But at the same time, the owners have opted for a twenty-first century approach to energy consumption, thus using the best of the past and the future.

PROJECT NAME:
River Cottages
LOCATION:
Chicago, Illinois
CLIENT:
Larrabee-Dickens Corporation
ARCHITECT:
Harry Weese & Associates: Harry Weese FAIA,
designer
PHOTOGRAPHY:
Hedrich-Blessing

River Cottages

Chicago, Illinois

Following in the Footsteps —Chicago Today

Just as the Chicago architects of the late 19th century could provide better housing through the use of light and space that technology allowed, Harry Weese uses technology to enhance multiple-housing units on a river front site in Chicago today. By using metals that did not exist before the Industrial Revolution—stainless steel and aluminum—he provides individual units within the same structure the opportunity to enjoy outdoor terrace spaces, and to have ample light for the long winter months, plus access to a recreation area in their own front yard.

You might say that technology has changed the way we design housing and the way we use the site. In designing the RIVER COTTAGES, Harry Weese was faced with a specific challenge. Because of an existing sewage system, the site had been deemed unsafe to build on; it was also extremely small. However, with the river frontage, it was also desirable. The solution Harry Weese found was to design an extremely light structure using STO (artificial stucco),

You might say that technology has changed the way we design housing and the way we use the site. In designing the RIVER COTTAGES, Harry Weese was faced with a

steel frame and turn-coated stainless steel on the sloping facades. Many of the components are prefabricated—again, a process of industrialization—and their use in different configurations provides not only interest, but a unity of design concept throughout the project

Another aspect of this design to consider is the amount of light the window areas allow into the interior. Before the Industrial Revolution and the advent of central heating and air-conditioning, window areas of this size would not have been practical. But now, with technology, you have vertical living space on an ''undesirable'' site with ample light and access to recreational spaces.

PROJECT NAME:
U.S. Embassy Housing
LOCATION:
Tokyo, Japan
CLIENT:
U.S. Dept. Office of Foreign Buildings
ARCHITECT:
Harry Weese & Associates: Harry Weese FAIA
PHOTOGRAPHY:
Mitsuo Matsuoka

U.S. Embassy Housing

Tokyo, Japan

*Americans Abroad—
Chicago Exported*

designing and building government housing overseas involves problem solving on a number of levels. When Harry Weese and Associates undertook the UNITED STATES EMBASSY HOUSING complex in Tokyo, all aspects of the design were subject to review by the "guidance committee" of the Tokyo

final design is a structure supported on friction piles and caisson foundations with a cladding of 1'' thick stucco panels, applied in situ, separated by 4'' side neoprene gaskets on all 4 edges. Mock-ups of this design were tested in laboratories both in Chicago and Tokyo prior to building.

When one examines the final result of this technological research, it becomes obvious that not only has Harry Weese and Associates achieved an overall design that is in keeping with the urban scape of Tokyo, but also one that provides space, light, recreational areas, child care, community facilities and adequate housing—173 new dwelling units—all on a 12-acre site.

Municipal Government. This committee reviewed zoning, firetruck access, sunshine/shadow regulations, height and density requirements, on site parking requirements as well as monitoring neighbor hearings. In addition to these criteria, the stresses of typhoons and earthquakes had to be considered as part of the structural loads.

The structural problems were solved with the help of Dr. Tooshiko Kimura. The

PROJECT NAME:
Cedar-Riverside
LOCATION:
Minneapolis, Minnesota
CLIENT:
Cedar Riverside Associates, Inc.
ARCHITECT:
Ralph Rapson & Associates, Inc.: Ralph Rapson
FAIA, Richard B. Morrill, Kay M. Lockhart
C. Michael Niemeyer, Timothy L. Stone, Frank
Nemeth, Greg Haley, James McBurney
AWARDS:
Honor Award for Urban Design Concepts,
1974—U.S. Dept. of Housing and Urban
Development; First Honor Award (for Cedar
Square West), 1975—AIA; Bartlett Award Design
for Handicapped (for Cedar Square West),
1975—AIA; Honor Award, 1976—Minnesota
Society AIA

Cedar-Riverside

Minneapolis, Minnesota

Urban Renewal—A "New-Town-Within-A-City"

these models show the overall urban renewal concept of creating a new vital community within central Minneapolis—a new-town-in-town project. It's been made possible by a collaboration of national, state, local and private financing. The next photographs show CEDAR-RIVERSIDE, the first new structures which contain some 12,500 dwelling units, and are meant to house 30,000 people.

Naturally, the project has not been a stress-free undertaking for the firm of Ralph Rapson and Associates, but the architects believe in the philosophy that, "out of coordinated planning, representing all aspects of community design, a heterogeneous community will evolve that wishes to live close to major educational, health and cultural institutions." In order to

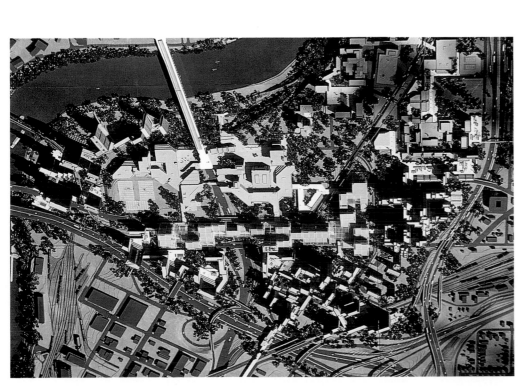

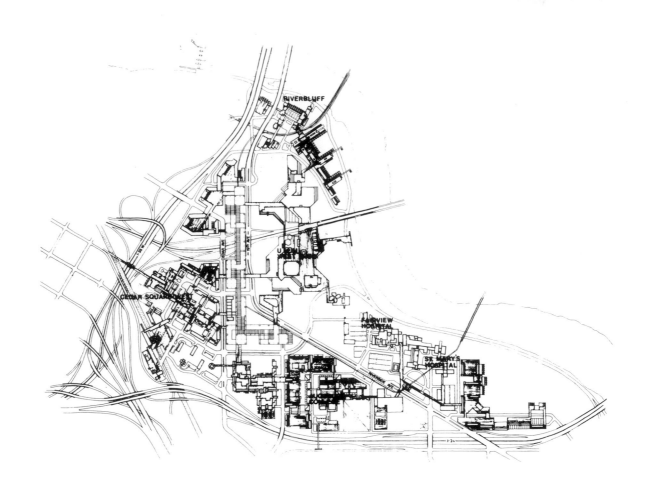

achieve this, however, the designers spent multiple hours in political "lobbying" and in finding ways to physically incorporate high-rise, medium-rise and low walk-up buildings into one overall scheme.

The designers were working toward a goal of construction designed at a human scale. To integrate the different configurations of housing units they adopted a reinforced concrete structural system using both cast-in-place and slip form techniques, and precast and post-tensioning concrete.

The possible monotony of these exterior walls were broken up and made interesting with a variety of materials—"dri-vit" systems and modular brick.

Another aspect of innovative technology in the planning stages, is a system of climate controlled walkways to link all principle areas. Landscaped rooftop

plazas are another idea the designers hope to see in the final design. Certainly, the architects have been responsible for creating an urban environment that is accessible and attractive for the residents of the low and moderate income housing that makes up half of the completed Cedar-Riverside complex.

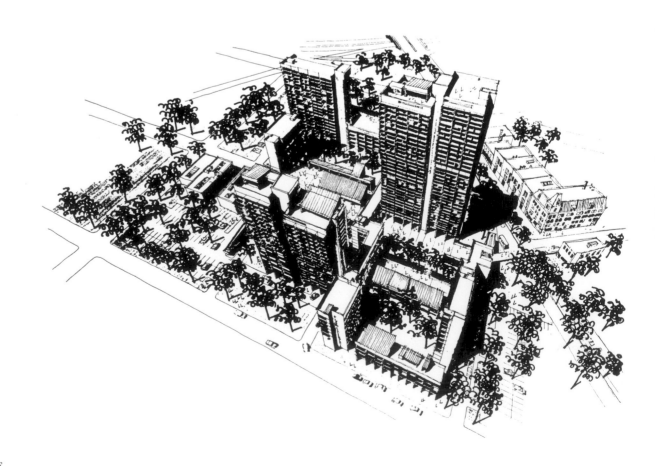

PROJECT NAME:
The Park
LOCATION:
Brookline, Massachusetts
CLIENT:
Myerson/Allen & Co.
ARCHITECT:
CBT/Childs Bertman Tseckares & Casendino Inc.:
Richard Bertman FAIA, Robert Brown,
Robert Michel
PHOTOGRAPHY:
Nick Wheeler
AWARDS:
Renaissance '88 Merit Award, 1988—Remodeling
Magazine; Project of the Year Award, 1988—
Builder Magazine; Award for Excellence in
Architecture, 1988—New England Regional
Council; Award for Excellence in Housing,
1987—Boston Society of Architects

The Park

Brookline, Massachusetts

Victorian Charm & the Automobile

In contrast to Cedar-Riverside, THE PARK, in Brookline, Massachusetts makes no claims to providing low and middle income housing. The Park, a restoration of the buildings of the Free Hospital for Women, is

situated in an affluent neighborhood and provides luxury condominiums and rental apartments. The major problem in technological expertise and materials, was how to repair and redesign the four salvaged buildings into 70 rental apartments —and how to construct 16 new condominiums that could be integrated into a total complex. The original hospital, of course, dates from around 1890. And in 1890 you might have needed a stable for the horses, but not parking spaces for the automobile.

CBT/Child Bertman Tseckares & Casendino Inc. solved part of the problem by constructing a reinforced concrete

HUNNEWELL HOUSE
ENTRY LEVEL

THE HYAMS

ENTRY LEVEL

research—by going back to Frederick Law Olmstead's original landscape plan—they were able also to reconstruct many of the elements that once made this site so attractive. Berming is one of the best examples.

Certainly this amalgamation of the old and the new into one cohesive unit has added to the esthetic quality of the neighborhood and preserved the open human-scale character. Tearing down this complex to make way for a new high-rise parking garage beneath the new condominium complex. And although parking for the existing buildings had to be surface asphalt paved areas, these are broken up by terracing. By use of some archival

SECTION

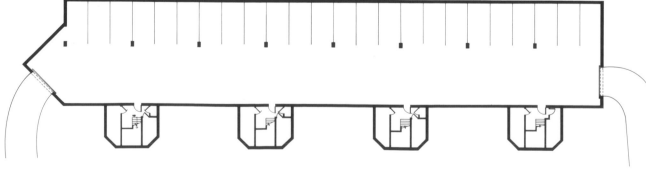

BASEMENT/PARKING

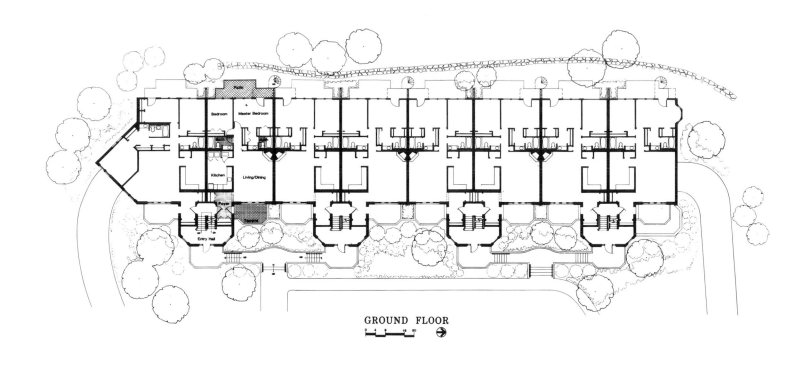

GROUND FLOOR

apartment house would have diminished the neighborhood and destroyed charming Victorian buildings that have been successfully integrated, once again, into the fabric of the community.

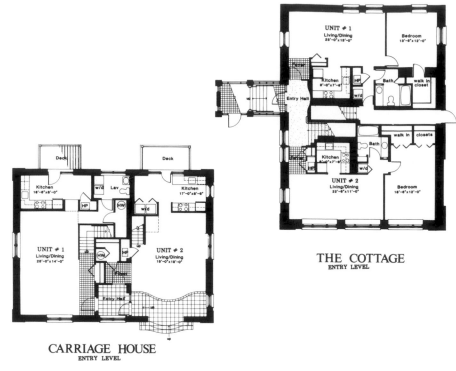

THE COTTAGE
ENTRY LEVEL

CARRIAGE HOUSE
ENTRY LEVEL

PROJECT NAME:
Seinpost Residence
LOCATION:
Amsterdam, The Netherlands
CLIENT:
Seinpost B.V. Dordrecht
ARCHITECT:
Architectenburo Cees Dam BNA BNI
PHOTOGRAPHY:
Jan and Fridtjof Versnel, Erik Hesmerg

Seinpost Residence

Amsterdam, The Netherlands

From Where the Ships Were Alerted

Seinpostduin is the highest point on the dunes on the Scheveningen coast. On this site (from where the ships used to be alerted to danger), a luxury apartment house has been constructed. Each and every apartment has a conservatory with a sliding glass opening that allows a view of the sun and sea.

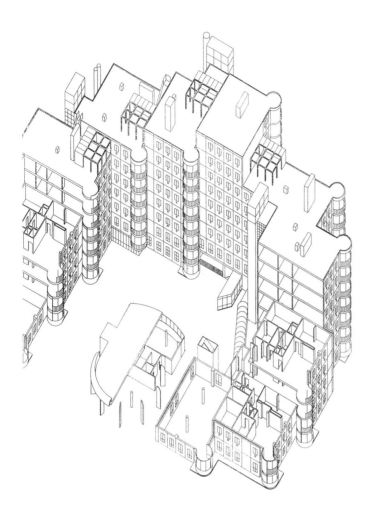

This apartment complex—the SEINPOST RESIDENCE—designed by Architectenburo Cees Dam, used these conservatories as a design element, and designed them as round towers reminiscent of old lighthouses in their fenestration and materials. The materials of the complex as a whole are in a nautical style—white concrete cladding panels, white semi-gloss glazed tiles, and white enameled aluminum door and window frames. The orientation and design of the towers also takes the views into consideration. The nine story towers are at the rear of the site and scale down to five stories toward the beach and sea.

The complex is horse-shoe shaped; in the middle of the inner court, is a restaurant open to the public. Parking and storage are both accommodated in an underground car park and storage area that takes up the basement level of the entire site. All the comforts of modern living are included in this apartment building, including luxury interiors—marble floors or wall-to-wall carpeting, soundproofing, and

insulation against the winter weather (through the use of double glazing). From this giant complex which replaces the historical signaling post, the tenants can still watch the sea and be alert to danger themselves, without braving the elements.

//

RECREATIONAL SPACES

" . . . 'gathering' is a main theme."

FUMIHIKO MAKI, MASATO OHTAKA
"Some Thoughts On Collective Forms"
Structure in Art and in Science

Perhaps one of the main ways in which the Industrial Revolution has influenced recreational spaces is in the need for and use of such spaces. The technology and innovations since the mid-1800s have allowed us to have more leisure time. We also have the transportation facilities to make use of our leisure time away from home. To this end, entertainment industries of many types have developed—parks, playgrounds, zoos, sports facilities, concert halls. All places to spend our time and improve our minds and bodies. Before technology, the average person would spend his time waking to sleeping making a living or a home; leisure time was only for the wealthy. Today, the pastimes of the more privileged can be made accessible to the average citizen.

In fact, almost everyone has access to some sports facility or complex. Governments often finance new installations, and following sports teams has become a worldwide national pastime.

■ STADIUMS, SWIMMING POOLS & SPORTS COMPLEXES

Physical fitness, holistic medicine—the integration of the physical, intellectual and spiritual life—are, however, not just concepts of our life in the twentieth century. These concepts are as old as civilization. Games, sports and places in which to play them are an ancient concept.

For example, on the site where Mexico City now stands, the Aztecs built the Great Temple of Tenochtitlan, and part of the temple complex was a ball court, directly aligned on the axis of the Great Temple. One can speculate on the symbolism of this, but one undeniable fact remains; a ball court was important in the educational and spiritual life of the Aztecs.

Perhaps one can conclude from this that the Industrial Revolution has not affected man's need for, nor ability to build gymnasia, swimming pools, ball courts and the like. This is not entirely true. The Industrial Revolution has given us the materials and techniques to build our sports complexes for use in all weather, and the ability to build more structures through the use of low-cost materials and efficient, less labor-intensive building techniques.

In many ways, both materials and artistic form have also influenced the design of theaters and concert halls throughout history.

■ THEATERS & CONCERT HALLS

In primitive villages an area might be set aside as the "dance circle," and in ancient Greece and Rome amphitheaters were a part of a city in the same way as the temples and the "agora"; it was a necessary part of their daily lives. It was a place of meeting, of assembly, of entertainment and, of course, a place of learning or propaganda.

In the Middle Ages, the town square (usually opposite the cathedral) served the function of a theater. Passion plays and occasional strolling players were the main attractions. During the Renaissance, theaters and theater companies became more organized, music became more secular and the operas produced required structures to accommodate them. The outdoor theater had evolved into an architectural form that required acoustics —technology became a part of the theater design.

The invention of motion pictures required a further adaptation: movie theaters, projectors, complex screen configurations, sophisticated sound systems and "3D." Each invention required new design techniques, but the function of a theater is still to provide a place for the entertainment and for new work and performers to be heard.

In its early beginnings, the stage was a packed earth circle and the audience perched on a rising slope. But with today's technology, it's possible to expand on that simple and basic concept and create structures that not only allow esthetic performances, but that are esthetic in themselves. Today, it's also possible to expand entertainment into the animal world—zoos, aquariums and the like.

■ ZOOS, AQUARIUMS & HISTORICAL PARKS

Zoos have been in existence since 4500 B.C. when pigeons were kept in captivity in what is now Iraq. About 1150 B.C. the Empress of China, Tanki, built a marble "house of deer," and Alexander the Great kept sending back to Greece the exotic animals he found on his military expeditions.

As for aquariums...there is some record that the Sumerians kept fish in artificial ponds. Certainly the Chinese were into breeding carp. The ancient Romans were the first to keep marine life by constructing ponds kept filled with seawater by cutting channels to the ocean. But, until the relationship between animals, oxygen and plants became known and understood in the middle of the 1800s, aquariums, as we know them today were not in existence. It took technology to perfect the exhibits and areas for scientific study that we enjoy today.

Possibly, one can say that historical parks have been around forever since, for the most part, the idea behind them is either to preserve the natural environment or to preserve an ancient site of historical significance. We like to see these places from the past in the same way we like to study exhibits in museums and books in libraries. Being reminded of what we once were and where we came from keeps us aware of where the future might take us.

Certainly from an environment standpoint all of these so-called "recreational" areas are also areas of scientific study. We study past cultures to find out how they failed (if they're no longer in existence) or how they evolved into the culture of today. We study animals, marine life and the natural environment to find out how and in what ways the pollution from technology is affecting our lives—and our future. Then, we attempt to develop technology that will give us innovative ways of preservation and ideas for housing these life forms—and ourselves. As technology evolves and more and more innovation requires that we work fewer hours and have more time for recreation, the need for recreational facilities will increase.

PROJECT NAME:
Physical Education Fieldhouse
LOCATION:
Duluth, Minnesota
CLIENT:
University of Minnesota
ARCHITECT:
The Leonard Parker Associates: Leonard S. Parker,
principal-in-charge
PHOTOGRAPHY:
Balthazar Korab
AWARDS:
Award of Excellence, 1977—American Institute of
Steel Construction; Merit Award, 1975—MSAIA;
Grand Award, 1975—Minnesota Consulting
Engineers Council

Physical Education Fieldhouse

Duluth, Minnesota

*Earth Sheltering—New
Uses for Old Technologies*

the use of earth sheltering, constructing a major portion of this structure below ground for energy conservation is only one of the innovative (albeit historic) technologies used by The Leonard Parker Associates in the PHYSICAL EDUCATION

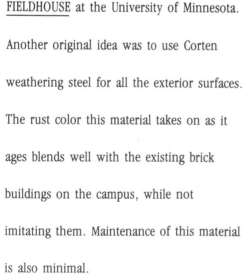

FIELDHOUSE at the University of Minnesota. Another original idea was to use Corten weathering steel for all the exterior surfaces. The rust color this material takes on as it ages blends well with the existing brick buildings on the campus, while not imitating them. Maintenance of this material is also minimal.

The roof system of the fieldhouse is a skew-chord truss supported on inclined trussed steel piers. The canted wall reduces the clear span of the truss and, of course, makes the structure more economical. Under this fortress-like structure of steel and earth all the playing fields lie snug from the blizzards and storms much like the sod houses of the earlier settlers.

This below grade surfacing also allows this new structure to connect more easily with existing circulation systems in the physical education complex. The architects were able to use the best of the old with new technologies to create a campus symbol that visually speaks of strength, discipline and power—and of innovative problem solving.

Municipal Baseball Stadium

Bayamon, Puerto Rico

PROJECT NAME:
Municipal Baseball Stadium
LOCATION:
Bayamon, Puerto Rico
CLIENT:
City of Bayamon
ARCHITECT:
Torres Beauchamp Marvel: Thomas S. Marvel,
architect; Hernandez & Hernandez, structural
engineers; Victor Garcia & Associates, mechanical
and electrical engineers
PHOTOGRAPHY:
Gilamiaga Architectural Photography
AWARD:
Honor Awards Program, 1978—AIA

*A Cable-Hung Protection
from the Sun & the Rain*

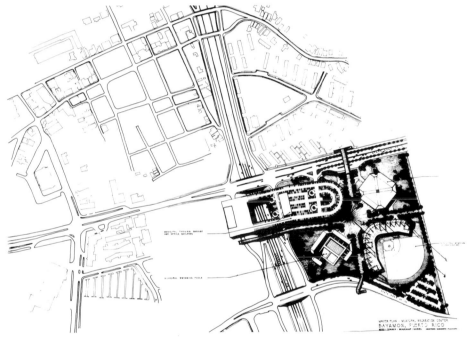

In the balmy weather of Bayamon, Puerto

Rico, protection from the sun and the rain

is the major consideration. With that

in mind, Thomas S. Marvel of

Torres.Beauchamp.Marvel selected this

cable-hung roof structure as the most

economical and the most appropriate for the

MUNICIPAL BASEBALL STADIUM.

The roof extends out 96 feet beyond

the supporting columns providing the

maximum shelter for the fans. The steel

Stadiums, Swimming Pools & Sports Complexes   43

beams are hung with 2'' cables, looped

upward over the columns and downward on

the rear through struts which are anchored

into the footings of the columns. Tension

pulls on compression members both

horizontally and vertically and thus

minimizes the bending moments. The

structure was tested for winds of 150 mph

at Virginia Polytechnic Institute, and the

resulting additional cable tie downs on the

front face add a further dimension to the

sense of draw-bridges and medieval towers.

There is nothing medieval about the

concept of this structure, however, and to

reinforce his concept, the architect visited

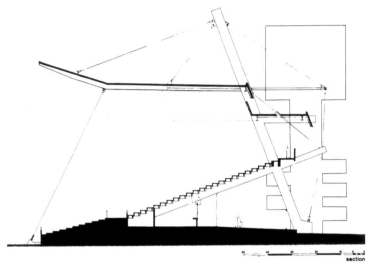

section

the Brooklyn Bridge during the schematic

design phase. In point of fact, The Roebling

Wire Rope Company supplied the same cable

connectors and cables for this structure and

for the Brooklyn Bridge.

Functionally, this reinforced concrete

stadium works well for spectators in a mild

climate, and certainly, the sense of play

expressed in the structure, plus the

enclosing form of the plan, surely contribute

to the fans enjoyment of the game.

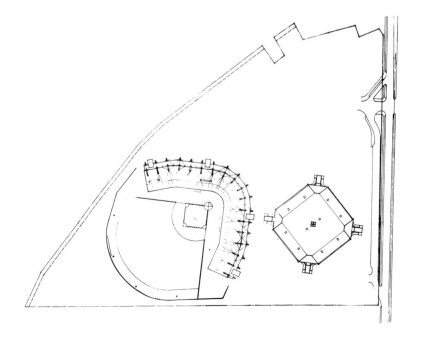

PROJECT NAME:
Recreational Facilities Building
LOCATION:
Carbondale, Illinois
CLIENT:
Southern Illinois University
ARCHITECT:
Ralph Rapson & Associates, Inc.: Ralph Rapson
FAIA, Richard B. Morrill, Kay M. Lockhart
AWARD:
Honor Award, 1976—Minnesota Society AIA

Recreational Facilities Building

Carbondale, Illinois

In the Greek Tradition

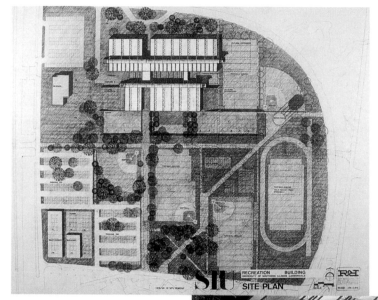

in the RECREATIONAL FACILITIES BUILDING at Southern Illinois University, the architects of Ralph Rapson & Associates have created a building in the Greek tradition of housing baths, dressing rooms, storerooms, a "wrestling ground" and other facilities where athletes can run, wrestle, box, or play ball games. Even the restful near symmetry of the plan of the building brings to mind the calm, classical order of the

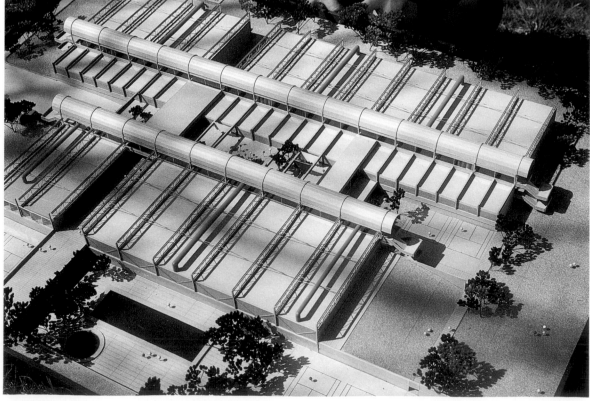

ancient world. The elevations and interiors, however, are a different story.

This building does not speak of ancient worlds as you approach the exterior

metal trusses presented as a major design element of this building that houses an Olympic swimming pool, three gymnasiums, an open interior court, handball and squash

courts, locker rooms, exercise rooms (for wrestling, fencing, boxing and judo), television, radio and game rooms, and student and faculty offices. All of this is in a building that totally integrates the architectural, structural and HVAC systems and succeeds in reducing heating and air conditioning costs.

Cost was a major factor in the design of this building—both maintenance cost and initial costs. Try to imagine this building in traditional materials and building techniques. The cost would be prohibitive and the time factors staggering; the entire complex was

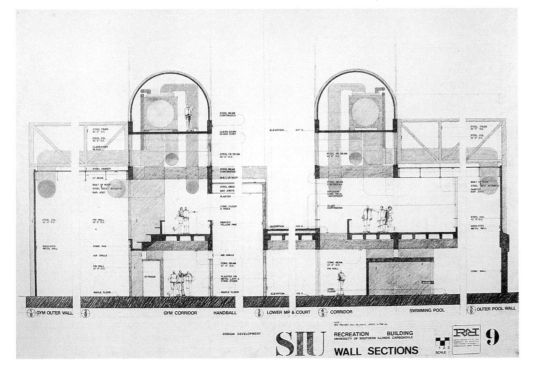

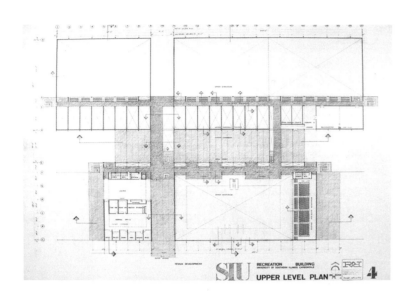

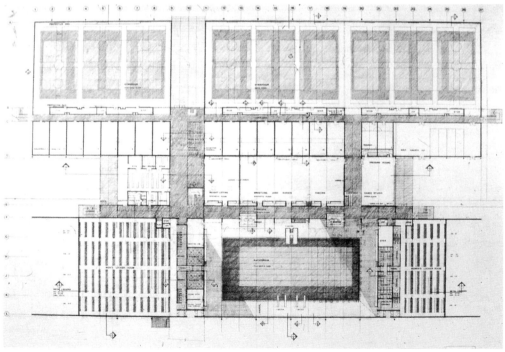

completed in sixteen months. In the design of this beautifully functional athletic structure with its jaunty exposed structural materials, the architects have created an environment that is not only attractive and functional, but one which can help to instill discipline, purpose, competitiveness and pride in accomplishment.

PROJECT NAME:
Tennessee State Amphitheatre
LOCATION:
Knoxville, Tennessee
CLIENT:
State of Tennessee
ARCHITECT:
McCarty Holsaple McCarty, Inc.: Doug McCarty,
architect
PHOTOGRAPHY:
David Luttrell
AWARD:
Award of Excellence, 1982—Tennessee Society of
Architects

Tennessee State Amphitheatre

Knoxville, Tennessee

In the Tradition of the Crystal Palace

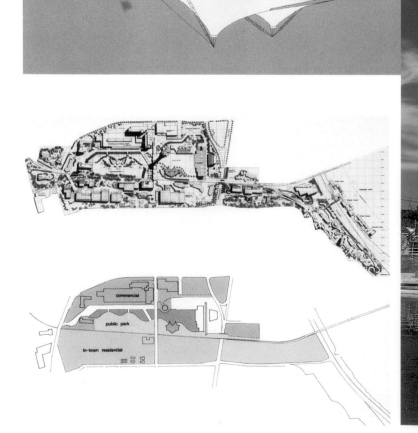

With its fluid wing-like shapes hovering over the audience like a giant butterfly, the TENNESSEE STATE AMPHITHEATRE became the technological design showpiece of the 1982 World's Fair in Knoxville, Tennessee in much the same way as the Crystal Palace was the showpiece of the Great Exhibition in London in 1851. But, whereas

prefabricated iron and glass were used in 1851, fiberglass fabric structures are what the architects, McCarty, Bullock & Holsaple, chose to execute their design solution in 1982.

The inherent problem they were faced with during design development was how to create an outdoor theater that would protect the audience and the performers from the elements, but still allow them to be a part of the natural environment. The tent-like structures seemed to be the perfect design solution.

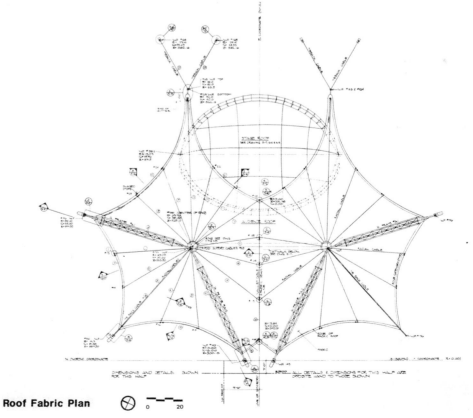

Roof Fabric Plan

To create the seating space, they bermed an area between the lake and the walkways, and located a reinforced concrete building under the berm to house the dressing rooms, storage and other support areas. Two vomitories connect these areas to the stage.

The stage itself is covered with its own fabric structure which has acoustical provisions as well as a lighting and sound

system. The fabric covering for the stage is a saddle-shaped tent stretched over a cable network that creates a proscenium arch. Seven steel cables were constructed between two opposing arches to form a stable structure.

The roof assembly over the audience was more complex to design and erect and uses two mirror image "tents" attached to support rings suspended from structural A-frames. This large tension structure is, in fact, trussed steel supporting masts and cables that are positioned on the outside of the "Teflon" coated fabric. Acoustics have also been given adequate consideration in this structure and, as the design challenge, proposed, it is possible to enjoy the performance on this unique stage, while still being a part of, and enjoying the natural surroundings. World's fair architecture has gone beyond mere exposition and become a community resource.

PROJECT NAME:
Town Hall/Operahouse
LOCATION:
Amstel 1, Amsterdam, The Netherlands
CLIENT:
Municipal Amsterdam
ARCHITECT:
BV Architectenburo Cees Dam BNA BNI in
cooperation with Wilhem Holzbauer
PHOTOGRAPHY:
Thomas Delbeck and Markus Tedeskino

The Town Hall/
Operahouse

Amstel 1, The Netherlands

Two Forms—
Two Functions

Using a facade of marble-dressed, punched

through elements that hint of giant "flats"

from the stage itself, the architects of

Architectenburo Cees Dam have visually

identified the TOWNHALL-OPERA-HOUSE

(STADHUIS-MUZIEKTHEATER) in Amsterdam

as a performing arena. Working in

collaboration with Wilhem Holzbauer, the

designers have created a four story monumental space that incorporates an auditorium, a foyer, studios, support areas and various public spaces.

Adjoining this structure on the same site—and as part of the same complex—is the Town Hall. This L-shaped building incorporates registration spaces, public information areas, a motion picture theater,

fact, to hide the technologically advanced light bridges in the ceiling, the visual artist, Peter Struycken created a "star spangled" sky. Before and after the performance the hall is lit by 550 small bulbs.

The integration of these two monumental structures was not an easy task. The architects have accomplished it by using the performing space as the focal element and repeating the flat punched through motif in areas to orient, direct and surprise.

and a post office. The two structures are linked together by transparent roofed passages that fill in the space between.

Using such design elements as circular steel staircases to connect seating levels and also incorporating various art works—including a granite sculpture—the designers have integrated the new with the old. In

PROJECT NAME:
African Pavilion
LOCATION:
Asheboro, North Carolina
CLIENT:
State of North Carolina
ARCHITECT:
Hayes-Howell, Professional Association
PHOTOGRAPHY:
Rick Alexander

African Pavilion

Asheboro, North Carolina

Africa Under a Tent

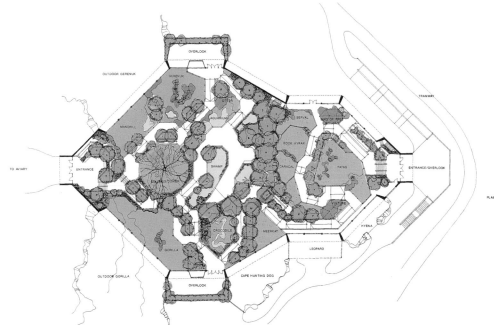

this structural system of three tension-supported, Teflon-coated fiberglass tents as a roof structure, brings to mind circus tents and safaris which is, indeed, appropriate symbolism for this AFRICAN PAVILION at the North Carolina Zoological Park in Asheboro, North Carolina. Designed by Hayes-Howell, this innovative system solves both the problem of providing exhibit space, and, at the same time, keeping the barriers and

CROSS SECTION

SCALE
0 5 10   20   50 FEET

enclosures as transparent as possible. It also allows enough natural illumination so no artificial light is needed.

The tent fabric is supported by one 60' and two 90' masts and the perimeter of the structure is a concrete compression ring supported on concrete walls and piers. Below the beam, the wall is laminated glass in hollow metal frames. Laminated glass is also used inside the exhibit area as the visitor is led by a carefully designed circulation plan through the entire exhibit.

To provide the keeper with access areas, loading docks and holding areas, the architects designed approximately 400' of tunnel space under the exhibit area in a reverse S-shape. The sloping site—40' from wooded hilltop to open plain—provides an area where exhibits can be both indoors and outdoors, and where the transparent glass walls (both inside and on the perimeter), allow the natural environment to be used as a backdrop for the animals and plant life.

Even the mechanical systems are designed with the latest in technological knowledge, and the temperature remains 15 degrees cooler inside even on the hottest

days. Walking—or using a wheelchair in this totally accessible space—through the exhibit of 200 animals and 3300 plants, the

designers have succeeded in visually and environmentally transporting you over thousands of miles to the "dark continent."

PROJECT NAME:
Primate Discovery Center—San Francisco Zoo
LOCATION:
San Francisco, California
CLIENT:
San Francisco Zoological Society
ARCHITECTS:
Marquis Associates: Robert B. Marquis FAIA,
Cathy Simon FAIA, Steve Perls,
Katherine Anderson
PHOTOGRAPHY:
Kirk Gittings / Steve Proehl
AWARD:
Architectural Award of Excellence, 1985—
American Institute of Steel Construction

Primate Discovery Center —San Francisco Zoo

San Francisco, California

A "Victorian" Education

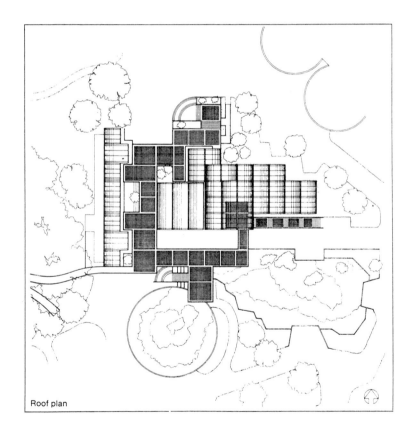

Roof plan

Using the materials of technology to help solve a problem (perhaps created in part by technology), the architects of Marquis Associates designed the PRIMATE DISCOVERY CENTER for the San Francisco Zoo. Designed around several species of primates, each species endangered, the complex attends to the diverse environmental needs of each species, and at the same time seeks to educate the public through such spaces as the "Nocturnal Center" and the "Discovery Hall" with its interactive computer controlled exhibits.

The tubular steel structure which comprises the main visual element of the

complex resembles a Victorian conservatory and the architects not only agree, they used the concept of a conservatory in the design solution. As the chief designer Cathy Simon states, "The Victorians used enormous glass pavilions to house exotic plants. We decided to use something similar to house exotic animals." In the case of the Primate House, however, much of the area is covered not by glass, but by vinyl-covered steel mesh.

In addition to the copper standing seam roof that also harkens back to the past, reinforced concrete is used to create the foundation, ramps, stairways and the multi-level viewing that allows the visitors to see the animals both at ground level and at "tree-top" level. The concept from the beginning has been to have the public interact with the animals and better understand the nature of primate behavior and conservation. By creating a total environment for these animals, the designers hope not only to allow the animals to breed for future reintroduction into the wild, but they also hope to educate the public to the need for conservation.

PROJECT NAME:
Aillwee Cave Visitors' Centre
LOCATION:
County Clare, Ireland
CLIENT:
Aillwee Cave Co. Ltd.
ARCHITECT:
A. & D. Wejchert: Danuta Kornaus-Wejchert and
Andrzej Wejchert, partners-in-charge;
Robert Carroll and Martin Carey, architectural
assistants
PHOTOGRAPHY:
A. & D. Wejchert, Henk Snoek, Pieterse Davison
International Ltd.

AWARDS:
Shannonside Environmental Award, 1979—
Shannonside; 'Plan' Building of the Year Award,
1980—Plan Magazine; An Taisce Commendation,
1981—An Taisce (National Trust of Ireland); 1980
''Europa Nostra'' 1982 Diploma; Commendation
by the RIAI (Gold Medal Jury for the period
1977-1979), 1986—The Royal Institute of
Architects of Ireland

Aillwee Cave Visitors' Centre

County Claire, Ireland

*An Underground
Experience*

from a distance, on the same plane, it's

difficult to identify the structure that

enclosed the entrance to the Aillwee Cave.

So successful were the architects,

A. & D. Wejchert, in using natural materials

as cladding for this reinforced concrete

structure, that the local grey limestone on

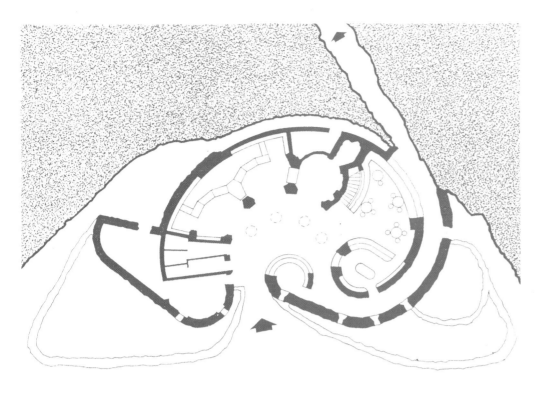

membrane between the concrete and the limestone.

The plan itself with its curved ramp that leads you into the cave entrance and the flowing organic forms of the spaces might even act as a decompression chamber for the visitors. To enter this structure is to go into a time warp and prepare yourself to view the flowing forms of the stalactites and the intimate pits dug by the bears millions of years ago. The entrance structure which the outside seems a part of the sloping hillside. This structure, AILLWEE CAVE VISITORS' CENTRE in County Clare, Ireland was commissioned by the owner of the cave to provide a way to regulate and control entry and exit from the Cave, a space to display information and educational material, a gift shop and a small restaurant

In order to achieve all this, however, the architects had to respect the integrity of the historical site and not detract from the natural landscape. They did this by incorporating elements of the landscape—the natural limestone—into the design. To use this material as cladding, however, it was necessary to use a damp-proof

nestles into, and grows out of the hillside in no way detracts from the visitor's experience. This integral structure reflects the timelessness of the barren hillside, the Atlantic and the underground wonders.

PROJECT NAME:
National Aquarium
LOCATION:
Baltimore, Maryland
CLIENT:
Bureau of Construction Management
ARCHITECT:
Cambridge Seven Assoociates: Peter Chermayeff
FAIA, principal-in-charge; Bobby Poole AIA,
project architect; Peter Sollugub, project designer;
Frank Zaremba, exhibit designer
PHOTOGRAPHY:
Steve Rosenthal
AWARDS:
Honor Award for Excellence in Waterfront Design,
1987—Waterfront Center; 16th Annual Award,
Architectural Category, 1979—Progressive
Architecture

National Aquarium

Baltimore, Maryland

A National Treasure Tank

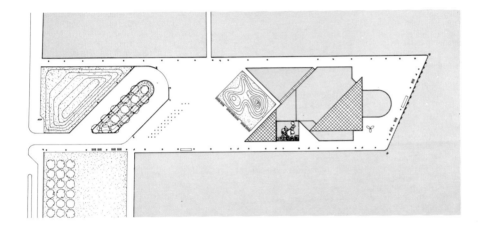

the NATIONAL AQUARIUM in the Baltimore

Harbor appears to be the superstructure of a

giant cargo ship, riding very low in the

water. Situated on the end of a pier, jutting

out into the harbor, the sense of movement

is palpable as one views the sweep of the

glass pyramids heading into the wind. On

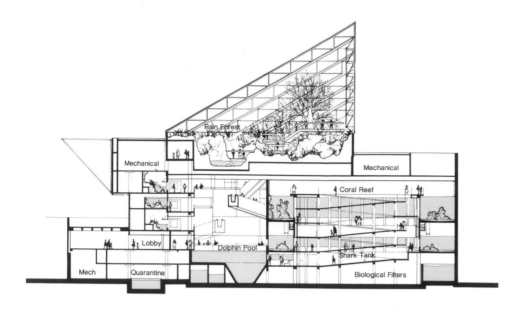

closer inspection, one can begin to identify the various elements that make up this complex of the various forms of sea life— the oval tanks, a rain forest with live animal life, and a children's tide pool area.

The designers of this entertaining and educational experience, the Cambridge Seven Associates, Inc. have used a wealth of structural, exhibition and media technologies to create spaces that entertain, educate and enchant the visitor. Perhaps the most important aspect of technology is the

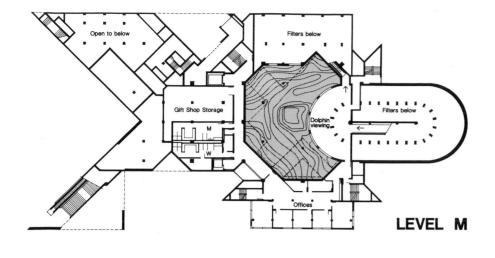

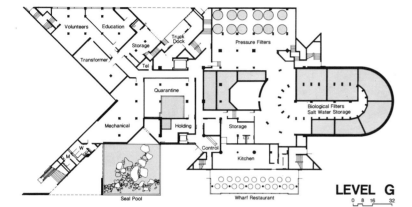

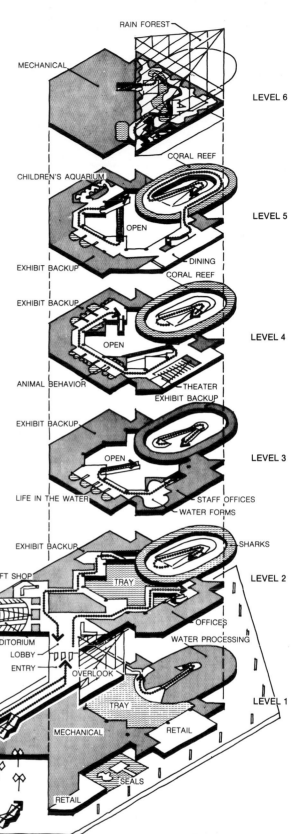

sophisticated life support system. This system manufactures sea water, has biological filtration and supplies ozone.

To house this life support system and the sea life, the designers used a cast-in-place structure with the structural steel and glass pyramids on the roof, custom designed for this specific building type with its inherent stresses. The acrylic glazing of the oval tanks has been achieved by the advances in the industry. Peter Chermayeff says that the new acrylic technology allowed them to "build 'walls' instead of windows, holding back huge volumes of water." When one considers the aquariums

built with windows to view the exhibit, the contrast is apparent.

The spaces of this aquarium are also of a new and different genre. Following a preordained circulation plan, the visitor is

led upward on moving walkways that bridge a central open space, allowing a view of the dolphin pool below. The walls contain exhibits and informational panels using photography and graphics. The only light is the reflected light from the exhibit pools and the sound is recorded sounds of the sea. Media forms assault the senses to intensify the experience.

At the top of the structure, under the glass pyramid is the rain forest with its live birds, reptiles and other animals. And leaving this steamy penthouse, counterpointed by the city scape of the Baltimore Harbor outside, one descends by a series of spiraling ramps into the inner core of the oval tanks, separated from the thousands of gallons of water by an acrylic wall.

From the entry wall of cylinders filled with bubbling blue water—the "water toys" —to the final exit, through the caverns and castles of this enchanted kingdom, the Cambridge Seven Associates, Inc. have used

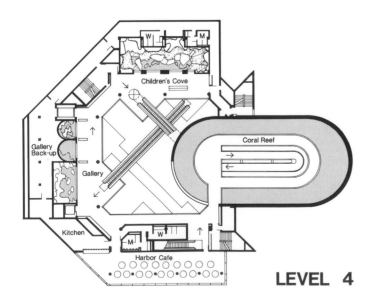

LEVEL 4

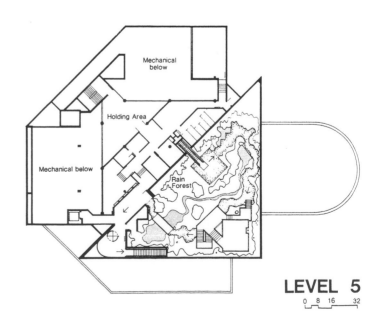

LEVEL 5

0   8   16   32

PROJECT NAME:
Monterey Bay Aquarium
LOCATION:
Monterey, California
CLIENT:
Monterey Bay Aquarium Foundation
ARCHITECT:
Esherick Homsey Dodge and Davis:
Charles M. Davis FAIA, principal-in-charge;
Linda Rhodes, project manager; Ruther &
Chekene, structural, civil and marine engineering
PHOTOGRAPHY:
Jane Lidz; EHDD; ESTO

AWARDS:
Award of Excellence, 1984—Portland Cement
Association Concrete Building; Honor Award,
1985—California Council AIA; Top Honor Award,
Current Project, 1987—Waterfront Center Awards
Program for Excellence on the Water; Honor
Award, 1988—AIA Monterey Bay Chapter;
National Honor Award, 1988—AIA; Regional
Award for Historic Preservation, 1984—California
Historical Society

Monterey Bay Aquarium

Monterey, California

Reviving Cannery Row

the challenge to Linda Rhodes of Rhodes/ Dahl and Charles Davis of Esherick Homsey and Davis—the designers of the MONTEREY BAY AQUARIUM—was how to recycle the old Hovden Cannery (a sardine-producing plant) into a modern aquarium. After a detailed study, they decided the building was too dilapidated to be usable, and only

retained the warehouse, the boilers (only visually reconstituted) and the chimneys (which serve only a historical and sculptural function).

The new structure, designed in the same industrial style as the original, seems almost a cross between a museum of Cannery Row and an aquarium. Using a concrete frame, wood and mineral fiber-cement corrugated siding for infill panels and wood trusses for the roof structure, and mineral fiber-cement shingles for roofing, the building almost replicates the old plant which is listed with the National Register of Industrial Places. To complete the menu of

materials, copper was used for the flashing and sprinklers, the piping is fiberglass and PVC with stainless steel connectors, and the steel windows and doors are epoxy coated. All materials are consistent with a project in the surf zone.

There were many problems inherent in building this rambling complex. Since 1/3 of the building is over a tidal zone, the heavy surf was a major problem. The heavy concrete footings, piers and concrete base structure had to be constructed during the

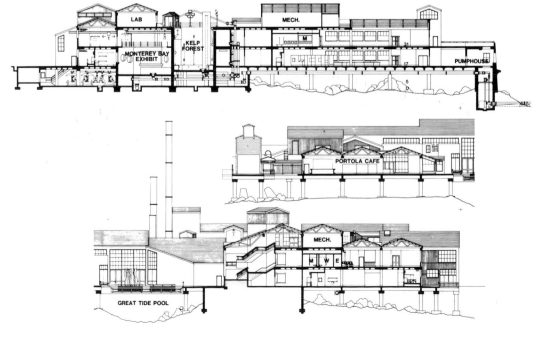

periods of low tides. And, of course, the problems of waterproofing systems and the development of methods to "build habitats for living critters that are non-toxic," were consistent concerns.

In this, the designers have succeeded brilliantly. The huge tanks that house the Kelp Forest and the Monterey Bay Exhibit rise several stories. The Kelp Tank holds 335,000 gallons of water and the Monterey Bay Tank holds 326,000 gallons. The acrylic exhibition windows manufactured by Mitsubishi Rayon of Japan, engineered to withstand the tremendous water pressure, go up to 15 feet high, 8 feet wide and are 7 ¼ inches this. Each of them weighs 2.73 tons.

The configurations of the tanks seem to immerse the viewer and enclose him in a

watery world, while still allowing him to remain dry and safe. Nearby the giant portholes allow views into smaller exhibits. In some, there are acrylic bubbles to lean into for an inside view.

Overhead, a procession of lifesize fiberglass sea mammals guides the visitor along the exhibits. The Sea Otter Tank provides fun and enchantment for visitors,

while providing a rescue service for orphaned pups. Outside and under the aquarium is a man-made tide pool that can be viewed from the deck or the edge of the tidal stair.

The technology of the exhibits has been carefully designed and controlled to provide both an educational and entertaining experience for the viewer, and to serve as a research facility for scientific personnel. At the same time, the aquarium, with its industrial ambiance, is a reminder of the innovative technologies that once existed when Cannery Row was more concerned with canning fish than exhibiting them.

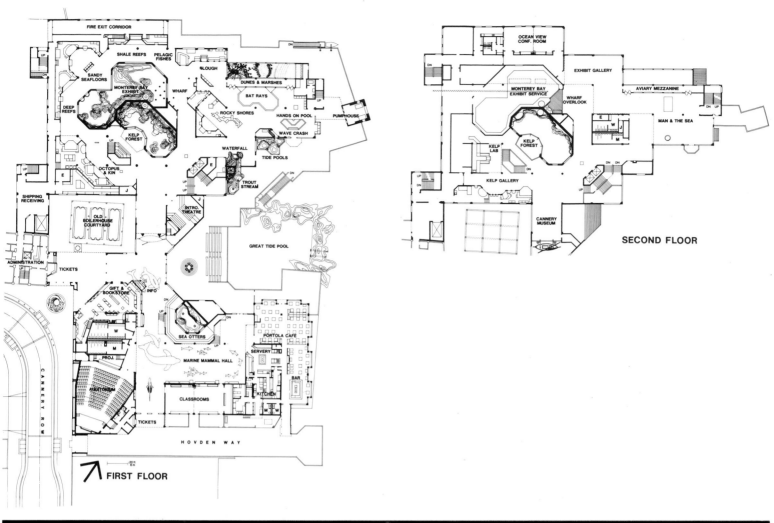

CHAPTER ///

INSTITUTIONAL ARCHITECTURE

''The plant grows from its seed. The characteristics of its form lie concealed in the potential power of the seed. The soil gives it strength to grow, and the outer influences decide its shape in the environment.''

ELIEL SAARINEN
Eliel Saarinen

While all these institutions—schools, universities, libraries, museums, seats of government, religious buildings, and health care facilities—were in existence before the Industrial Revolution, the philosophies underlying them have been altered by technology. First technology and industrialization, and now computerization have altered the administration and, in some ways, the import of these institutions. For the most part, however, all the innovations have contributed to the well-being, comfort and efficient use of these structures.

Schools, universities and health care facilities probably have been impacted by technology and computerization more than other institutions. However, all have benefitted from the innovations of advance technology.

■ SCHOOLS
Schools in one form or another have always existed, but the nineteenth century brought a further consolidation of national states and secularization of education, and new school systems needed to be developed to incorporate all these changes in the sociological structure—national school systems needed schools that stressed the sciences and reflected the new technological and commercial age. With the trend toward universal and public education, the existing educational structures —both philosophical and physical—were inadequate.

To accommodate these new trends, much research has been done over the decades, and new philosophies of education have been developed. Many of these philosophies stress activities that require equipment and spaces for the students to engage in exploratory activities. The days of students sitting quietly at desks, all in a row, dipping their pens in the ink well appear to be gone. Now, designers speak of ''learning environments'' and ''media centers.''

The advent of new materials—reinforced concrete, steel, aluminum, plastics—partially brought about this crisis and all these materials have been used to create learning environments that allow new and innovative curriculums to be taught. New elementary educational architecture provides computer laboratories and electronic media innovations. New materials and new inventions have created new innovative structural and interior solutions. The school as we once knew it has evolved into a more complex and technological form. Universities have also suffered technological growing pains.

■ UNIVERSITIES
The first universities were probably established in the 13th and 14th centuries. Before this, as an outgrowth of the monasteries, there were groups of students and professors who banded together for learning purposes, but it was not an institutional organizaton as such. There were no organized architectural spaces, designed as, and designated as, a ''university''—until Oxford and the University of Paris.

But, if you stop to consider the wealth of scientific knowledge that has been discovered in the intervening 700 years, it becomes apparent that the design of university buildings must be somewhat different than it was when the university concept came into being. Originally, the universities and colleges were designed around living spaces and a chapel. There were no scientific laboratories because there was no need. Today, the requirements for a university are entirely different.

Each year, along with new stadiums and student unions, libraries and classroom spaces, scientific and technical laboratories are being designed and built, often with large contributions from industry. Since the Industrial Revolution, a part of scientific and technological research has been carried on at university campuses. Amazing breakthroughs have been achieved.

But, along with the breakthroughs has come the thinking (a large and essential component of any university atmosphere) about both the efficacy and the morality of implementing these new advances, and there are always the legal implications as well. The examples of university architecture express both sides of the dilemma. The need to explore and create new scientific and technological breakthroughs is there. Side by side with this exploration, the need to evaluate where and when we use this knowledge is also a necessity.

Evaluation and exploration are two of the reasons libraries exist. We need to keep records of the discoveries of today. We need records of our accomplishments—and our failures.

■ LIBRARIES
We are all a product of our collective pasts— both remembered and un-remembered, both written and oral. Libraries are repositories for those recorded, treasured reminders and remnants of our cultures that we wish to pass on to future generations. In a way, perhaps, by displaying and studying the elements of our past that we treasure, we also pass on values and codes of conduct from generation to generation.

Beyond values and codes of conduct, however, inherent in libraries is the potential to educate one group of people about the lifestyles of other diverse groups of people. This is one way of unifying the world, contributing to the understanding between nations and building a true ''global'' sense among nations.

And, of course, there is the issue of recorded knowledge. If someone discovered something—a scientific invention, a new recipe, a path to take, or a new idea—who's to say anyone will remember when that person dies? Recorded knowledge is important. It keeps all of us from constantly re-inventing the wheel. It allows us to build on the knowledge of the past.

Today the library is not just a repository for written records. Libararies store media of all kinds. All forms of communication now seem to fall under the category of library acquisitions and facilities must be designed to protect these documents and also to allow the public to see and use them.

Museums are also structures and institutions that preserve the past for study and evaluation.

■ MUSEUMS

In churches, monasteries and universities, there have been collections (one might call them museums) since the Middle Ages. It's possible to speculate that the spoils and curiosities brought back by the Crusaders might be responsible for these early beginnings. Next, as the explorers began to sail off to far lands and circumnavigate the globe, royal collections began to be developed: providing consumption and viewing only for the privileged few of course. But, with the French Revolution and the opening of the Louvre to the public, the history of the museum changed. The British followed the French and national museums came into existence. Regional museums followed and museums also became devoted to special interests—art, science and natural history.

Each regional museum, of course, has a chance to store and/or exhibit those elements unique to the area. The inhabitants of the area have a chance to weigh and measure themselves in terms and ideals of the past, and perhaps of the present.

The function of a museum, as designers have found out when faced with the problem, is a combination of display and conservation. How do you exhibit the material to its best advantage, and yet protect and conserve it? Not an easy task. After all, one of a museum's main reasons for being is to use the collections as educational material. And to educate it must be seen—but not damaged by visitors or environmental conditions. So security and environmental controls are all important in museum design.

Beyond these aspects, museums can and should be community meeting places. The designers of these structures must keep in mind that these are not just exhibit rooms—although these elements, granted, play an important part in the design. These structures require places for people to meet and congregate. Because, in the final analysis, museums exhibit the actualization and culmination of ideas. Ideas—and the symbols that express those ideas—also play a large part in the design of seats of government.

■ SEATS OF GOVERNMENT

Since individuals began to band together for mutual protection and companionship there have been leaders—either chosen or imposed upon the group, snd with leaders, chiefs, emperors, and what have you, there's been the need to create special houses, places for residence, places for the group elders—the rulers—to meet. Thus, the formation of seats of government.

In today's societies with all their complexities, governments are needed to raise money to pay for highways, schools, libraries and a multitude of services. The list of government financed facilities is lengthy and complicated. Places to manage all these endeavors must, of course, be created and maintained. Laws must be enacted and enforced. The bureaucracy that develops is a part of government and needs to be housed.

The architect, however, must keep in mind that the process of government is, in many ways, made up of symbols. These symbols keep patriotism alive and contribute to pride in one's country and a willingness to sacrifice and contribute to the good of one's country. So in part, the architect must think symbolically when designing forms and spaces for seats of government. But, seats of government should also inspire. In many ways perhaps, they should be larger than life and they should also contain public spaces so the citizens can feel a part of the process of government, and they should use suitable materials.

As to what materials might be deemed suitable for a seat of goverment? Perhaps materials that symbolize permanence and security.

Choice of materials is also paramount in the design of religious buildings. Here, however, spiritual qualities and inspiration are the symbols to be expressed.

■ RELIGIOUS BUILDINGS

The requirements for an architectural space within which to worship would undoubtedly vary with each personal expression of worship. Yet, the architect is charged with the mission of finding some common denominator within congregations that will define the parameters and begin to clarify the form and visual expression of the building—and the religion.

From the beginnings of history, places of worship have been set aside, organized and constructed. Stonehenge, the great cathedrals, the Incan and Mayan Pyramids, the great temples of Egypt and Greece, Ankor Wat, the Meiji Shrine. The architect of today has a wealth of examples from which to draw inspiration, and a wealth of new materials to use in actualizing his inspiration and ideas.

When one stops to consider the great religious monuments of the past, they seem to have lasted because of their unique, and sometimes forward looking technology. It would seem, perhaps, that when cultures build for their God or Gods, they strive to build structures that will be permanent and that will outlast the human lifespan. Perhaps, today the goal is the same, and the materials and building techniques that the Industrial Revolution has given us, while not the time honored lasting stone of the past, certainly speak of the hopeful permanence of the future.

The future is also an important aspect of health care. Patients need to visualize a future of health, not sickness and pain.

■ HEALTH CARE FACILITIES

Today the hospital is a place for diagnosis, treatment and the study of the "machine"— the human body. It's also a place for healing and hope, not containment and despair.

Perhaps technology influences the design and building materials of medical architecture more than any other building form today. Nuclear medicine—to name just one branch of medical technology—has its own needs and parameters. To accommodate the new needs and parameters, architects and medical specialists must constantly confer with one another, exchange information and expertise, in order to design buildings that are useful to both the doctor and the patient.

Today, more and more attention is being paid to the psychological needs of the patient. Color, space—visual considerations that once were ignored—are now becoming part of the design program for hospitals, hospices and nursing homes. Designers and medical personnel are both paying attention to how the human mind affects the healing of the human body and health care facilities are being designed to heal the mind as well as the body.

The orientation of health care facilities is also changing. Doctors' offices sometimes take the place of outpatient emergency wards. Hospitals are crowded and, as the population ages, they will become more so. Architects and interior designers are being called upon to devise innovative solutions that will provide both physical and mental health care, taking into consideration the needs of medical technology, the medical staff and the patients. In this age of advanced and sophisticated technology, we have a wealth of materials and techniques at our fingertips which can help heal humanity.

PROJECT NAME:
Community School
LOCATION:
Ballincollig, County Cork, Ireland
CLIENT:
Dept. of Education
ARCHITECTS:
A. & D. Wejchert: Andrzej Wejchert and
Danuta Kornaus-Wejchert, partners-in-charge;
Paul Roche, architectural assistant
PHOTOGRAPHY:
Henk Snoek Photography Ltd.
AWARD:
Second Award in Community School Architectural
Competition, 1974—Dept. of Education

Community School

Ballincollig, County Cork, Ireland

Innovative Curriculum =
Innovative Architecture

the COMMUNITY SCHOOL AT BALLINCOLLIG, County Cork, Ireland is the outcome of a competition sponsored by the Department of Education of Ireland. As the result of a survey, Ireland adopted a comprehensive system to tie together the vocational and academic streams of their curriculums and provide greater community involvement in the schools. To do this, they needed 19 community school, and innovative thinking

to decide what physical form these new structures might take. Thus, the competition —"Design Ideas for Secondary Schools." The second prize in this competition went to A. & D. Wejchert. This prize led to a commission for the school illustrated. A. & D. Wejchert. This prize led to a commission for the school illustrated.

The modular plan of this concept was adapted to the needs of the site and the needs of the curriculum. The Humanities Departments are housed in the central core, the "Base Units" in the three units created by the semi-circular patterns, the Sciences in the shorter of the rectangular projections, the Practical Art Areas in the longer, and the Multi-functional Areas in the projecting pentagon. All of these geometric shapes are created by using a modular structural system of prefabricated structural roof and wall infill panels of GRP (glass reinforced polyester). Tubular steel columns supported by steel beams span the steel columns.

Color is used to relate the school to the surrounding landscape—the yellow gorse growing on the hillsides is a major theme in the three shades of yellow the architects selected. The geometric forms are used to orient the students to the various

activities and provide easy circulation. The importance of the siting and the environment are quite evident when it's realized that the school uses both natural daylight and natural ventilation. The maintenance and heat loss factors are low. Energy conservation is part of the total design concept in this school.

The advantage of this modular concept is its adaptability to other sites and other configurations. It's easy to assemble, multi-functional and inexpensive to build and maintain. And, considering the attractiveness of the interior environment, one would have to conclude that technology has contributed to the educational environment.

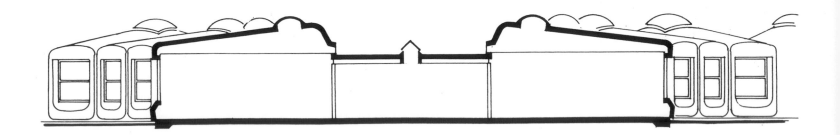

PROJECT NAME:
Elementary School
LOCATION:
Aviano, Italy
CLIENT:
Associazione Nazionale Alpini / U.S. Agency for
International Development
ARCHITECT:
Mitchell / Giurgola Architects
PHOTOGRAPHY:
Elio Ciol
AWARDS:
Distinguished Architecture Award, 1984—AIA
New York Chapter; Excellence in Design Award,
1983—New York State Association of Architects

Elementary School

Aviano, Italy

International Development

assisting in the program to help rebuild the

Friuli area of northeastern Italy that had

been devastated by an earthquake, Mitchell/

Giurgola Architects designed the

ELEMENTARY SCHOOL AT AVIANO, ITALY.

Part of a program sponsored by Associazione

Nazionale Alpini/U.S. Agency for International Development, the program for these schools is based on standard spacial requirements for the Italian education system.

The program for this particular school consists of six classrooms for 25 pupils each, a dining/conference area for 75, a main meeting area and support spaces. The designers grouped the classrooms around the central meeting area to allow orientation in two directions and access to the outside. Entrances are at either end of the long entry gallery which is across from the central space. The dining/conference area and the mezzanine which houses the teachers' offices are separated and located on the opposite side of the gallery.

This reinforced concrete structure has naturally used the latest in seismic research

to insure that should another earthquake strike, the structure will still stand. However, in this part of Italy it was felt that tradition should not be overshadowed by technology and the outside stucco finish has also been enhanced with a geometric design motif using the colored stones and marbles native to Italy. Physical life has

potentially been preserved with technology, and spiritual life and pride in one's heritage has been preserved by using indigenous and familiar materials.

PROJECT NAME:
3401 Walnut Street
LOCATION:
Philadelphia, Pennsylvania
CLIENT:
University of Pennsylvania
ARCHITECT:
Geddes Brecher Qualls Cunningham
PHOTOGRAPHY:
Bill Hedrich
AWARDS:
Tucker Award of Design Excellence, Building
Stone Institute, 1988; Honorable Mention,
Commerce/Tri-State Building Excellence Award,
1989

3401 Walnut Street

Philadelphia, Pennsylvania

Old Echoes, New Systems

On a roughly triangular site, Geddes Brecher Qualls Cunningham, Architects tackled the design problem of providing an entrance to the University of Pennsylvania "college green." The owners of the adjacent brownstones had successfully blocked the development of this site since 1973, and the architects were constrained by the shadow limitations imposed by these owners and by

the need to integrate the building into the visual and esthetic fabric of the neighborhood and the campus. At the same time, however, they also wanted to create a true "gateway" to the University of Pennsylvania campus.

The result, 3401 WALNUT STREET—a multi-use facility that houses office space, retail stores and a restaurant—is an L-shaped structure with playfully articulated arcades and two vertical circulation cores. The corner circulation core—the main entrance, the "gateway"—is arresting in its sculptural quality of projecting and intersecting solid geometrical elements.

Concrete floors built by use of a precast concrete form system (Filigree system) provided a system that required beams only in one direction and thus allowed four floors to be built within the height restrictions. This complex is also energy efficient, in that the heat generated by the computer room is used to heat the

office space in winter. The building is also completely handicapped-accessible.

The materials the architects chose are indicative of their careful research and sensitive design. They used both traditional limestone and the brick of the existing historical university buildings. Using the two materials to achieve both texture and color, the designers created a building that expresses the best of new techology and traditional values.

PROJECT NAME:
Hubert H. Humphrey Center
LOCATION:
Minneapolis, Minnesota
CLIENT:
University of Minnesota
ARCHITECT:
The Leonard Parker Associates: Leonard S. Parker, principal-in-charge; Francis Bulbulian, project manager; Gary Mahaffey, project architect; Stephan Huh, director of production; Ray Greco, designer
PHOTOGRAPHY:
Balthazar Korab, George Heinrich

AWARDS:
CUE Award, Humphrey Garden (designed with Siah Armajani, sculptor), 1989—Committee on Urban Environment; First Award of Achievement Concrete Products Association, 1988—Minnesota Masonry Institute; Honor Award for Excellence in Masonry Design and Construction, 1987—Minnesota Concrete and Masonry Contractors Association; Citation Award, 1986—American School and University Magazine

Hubert H. Humphrey Center

Minneapolis, Minnesota

Echoing Motifs

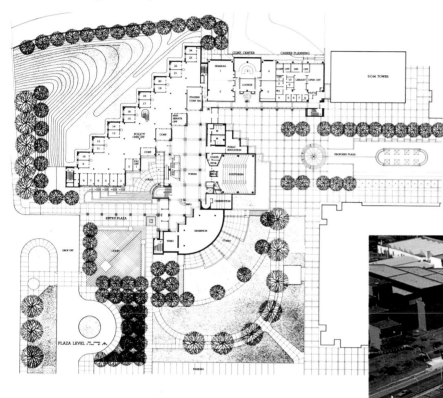

adjacent to the Law School on the University of Minnesota campus, The Leonard Parker Associates designed the HUBERT H. HUMPHREY CENTER. Although the stepped configuration on the northwest side complements the Law School, the building's masses as a whole bespeak a more

contemporary orientation and tradition. Very fitting, since one might say that a structure meant to express Hubert Humphrey's ideas and spirit should have a more open ambiance—an ambiance that invites the exchange of ideas, an interaction with fellow students and the public at large.

The central Forum, a large skylit three-story atrium, is the central circulation core of the building. With its descending theater-box like "pods" for seating opening off the staircase, this area invites one to exchange ideas, meet with friends and colleagues, then sit down and discuss the idea in depth while remaining in the center of activity. All this meets the Dean's request that the building maximize the opportunity for spontaneous interchange. At the same time, the "pods" provide viewing space for activities on the ground floor.

The building is energy efficient through its use of many of the same materials and techniques as the Law School, and also employs brick and precast concrete to visually integrate the building with the campus as a whole. As a monument to a man of vision and humanity, this reinforced

concrete building allows grandeur and

human scale to coexist side by side in a

tangible expression of a statesman's search

for global peaceful co-existence.

PROJECT NAME:
Hysolar Institute Building
LOCATION:
Stüttgart, Germany
CLIENT:
Saudi Arabia and Federal Republic of Germany
ARCHITECTS:
Behnisch & Partners: Frank Stepper and
Arnold Erhardt, project architects
PHOTOGRAPHY:
Behnisch & Partners / Christian Kandzia
AWARDS:
German Association Badenw-Württ Citation,
1987—German Architectural Association; Mies
Van der Rohe Prize, 1988—Flachglas AG; 8th
International Architecture Prize, 1988—Eternit AG,
Brussels; Hugo Häring Prize, 1988—German
Architectural Association

Hysolar Institute Building

Stuttgart, Germany

Restless Thrust, Parry & Flow

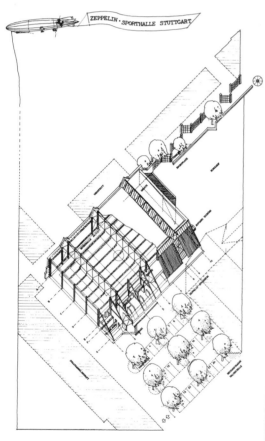

like the movement in Marcel Duchamp's "Nude Descending a Staircase," Behnisch and Partner's HYSOLAR INSTITUTE BUILDING at the University of Stüttgart never seems in repose. The metal components strive toward the heavens or seek to burrow into the

depths of the earth. The tensions that the structural elements create might be said to mimic the action of the hydrogen and oxygen this institute works with.

In point of fact, this institute is utilized in two ways—exploring methods of separating hydrogen and oxygen at relatively low cost, and also developing solar cells—both outgrowths of technology and the Industrial Revolution. The building materials are all the children of technology—steel columns, folded sheet aluminum, wood composition board, and asphalt—a collage of materials of the twentieth century creating a building of such freshness and tension that its small mass vibrates against the traditional fabric of the campus.

These materials were selected because of two vital design requirements; the building had to be completed quickly and on a low budget.

PROJECT NAME:
The Advanced Business Institute
LOCATION:
Palisades, New York
CLIENT:
IBM
ARCHITECT:
Mitchell / Giurgola Architects
PHOTOGRAPHY:
Mick Halles, P.G. Rolland

The Advanced Business Institute

Palisades, New York

Executive Training Center

many universities now offer training courses on a graduate level for executives. IBM offers training to the executives of their largest customers not at a university, but at the ADVANCED BUSINESS INSTITUTE in Palisades, New York. This center was conceived and designed by the architects of Mitchell/Giurgola on a 106-acre wooded site

the north contains the residential quarters and a fitness center. To the south, a three story wing has been designed for the educational and administrative functions.

To integrate the visual aspects of the building into the site, the architects have used steel, concrete and wood structural systems—each as they are appropriate to the functional requirements of the structure. The exterior materials—rose-colored molded brick, teak windows and trim and terne roof

where they have limited both vehicular circulation and parking to only portions of the site. This concept, of course leaves the majority of the site free for pedestrian traffic.

To capitalize on the tranquility of the site, the architects created a series of interconnecting ponds in the center of the site and all the architectural elements have access to and views of this man-made natural phenomena. The center building of the three incorporates the reception and dining functions and a serpentine wing to

are also in keeping with the peace and tranquility of the site. In the executed, landscaped complex, the architects seem to have achieved a sense of place that speaks of calm study and reflection in much the same way as an oriental summer palace.

PROJECT NAME:
Library Building of the Catholic University
LOCATION:
Eichstatt, Germany
CLIENT:
Stiftung der Katholischen Universitat Eichstatt
ARCHITECT:
Behnisch & Partner: Manfred Sabatke,
Christian Kandzia, Joachim Zurn, project
architects; Helmut Dasch, Jutta Schurmann,
Cornelia Theilig, Birgit Weigel and
Thomas Zimmerman, collaborators;
Sabine Behnisch-Staib, competition designer;
Martin Hühn, project manager; Hans Luz &
Partner, landscaping collaborators
PHOTOGRAPHY:
Behnisch & Partner / Christian Kandzia

AWARDS:
German Architecture Prize, 1987—Ruhrgas AG,
Essen; German Architects Association—Bavaria,
1987—German Architectural Association

The Library Building of the Catholic University

Eichstatt, Germany

A New Identity Among the Old—Nature & the Baroque

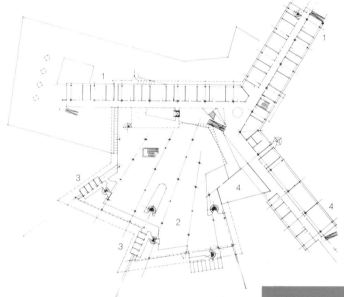

although the architects <u>Behnisch and Partner</u> state that the new <u>LIBRARY BUILDING OF THE CATHOLIC UNIVERSITY</u> at Eichstatt could not be built near the existing Baroque buildings of the campus because of the scale, there are elements in the new structure that are very much in keeping with the restless thrusts and movements

that mark the Baroque period. Granted the Baroque deals with curvilinear form and the Library Building is angles and planes, but the exuberance is there, the forms seeming never at rest and always in search of new configurations.

In materials and building techniques, however, this building is a product of the age of technology. In the aluminum, reinforced concrete, steel and glass, this structure expresses the searching inherent in library research and scholarship. It also expresses and provides space for the newer retrieval and research tasks that are a part of the library fabric of today's technology. Perhaps the loose configuration of forms also expresses the multi-media approach to information today; there's not one form of

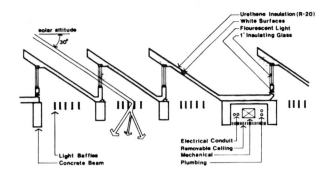

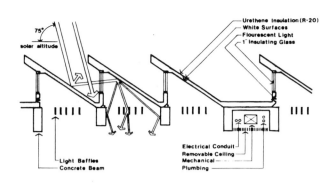

Clerestory Design- Winter Solstice

Clerestory Design- Summer Solstice

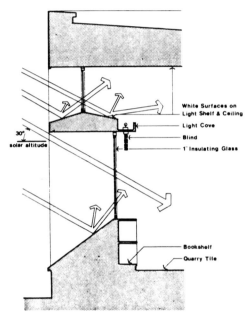

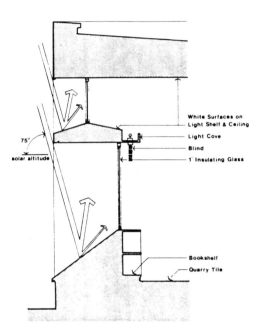

Light Shelf Design-Winter Solstice

Light Shelf Design- Summer Solstice

energy in commercial buildings.

Using a combination of heavily insulated walls and roof, masonry "mass" walls to maintain constant temperatures, double-glazing on the windows, light shelves and light-colored roofing to reflect sunlight into the clerestory space above the ceiling, and a baffle system below each clerestory to diffuse light, the architects created a building that uses natural light entirely during the daylight hours. The roof and wall apertures provide 100 percent of the building's light requirements and selectively admit some light during the winter for passive heating. What lighting is needed comes from fluorescent strip lights which have been integrated into the ceiling design.

The exterior material (white granite) comes from the local quarry and is in keeping with the cladding on the other City Center Buildings. The structure is a combination of concrete columns, steel frame and steel deck with exposed beams and grouted masonry infill. The sawtooth clerestories on the roof are an integral feature of the solar design, and they add interest to the simple, functional silhouette of the building.

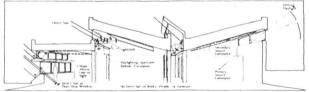

SUNLIGHTING

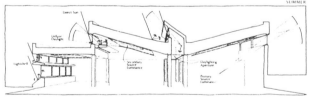

DAYLIGHTING

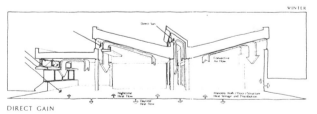

DIRECT GAIN

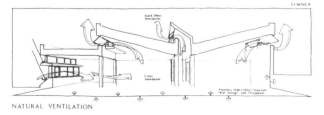

NATURAL VENTILATION

This functional silhouette was an outgrowth both of the program requirements and a solid granite substrata that limited excavation and pushed the architects to design the building in three stepped wings. This configuration worked well with the client's requirements of flexibility, openness and accessibility. It also allowed the designers to create a building that could be naturally lighted through both its orientation and the special details carefully worked into the design.

PROJECT NAME:
Grande Louvre
LOCATION:
Paris, France
CLIENT:
Etablissement Public du Grande Louvre
ARCHITECTS:
Pei Cobb Freed & Partners
PHOTOGRAPHY:
Koji Horiuchi, S. Couturier, Serge Hambourg
AWARDS:
Le Syndicat de la Construction Métallique de
France Prix Special, 1988; European Convention
for Constructional Steelwork Design Award, 1989;
L'Association de Ingenieurs- Conseils de Canada
Prix d'Excellence, 1989; Prix Spécial Grands
Projets Parisiens, Le Moniteur L'Equerre d'argent

Grande Louvre

Paris, France

A Connecting Form & Focus

I.M. Pei & Partners converted the former parking lot for the Ministry of Finance into the new Cour Napoleon that forms the plaza atop the GRANDE LOUVRE. The GRANDE LOUVRE is the outcome of years of study as to how the three separate wings of the Louvre might be modernized, connected, expanded and integrated into the transportation systems of Paris.

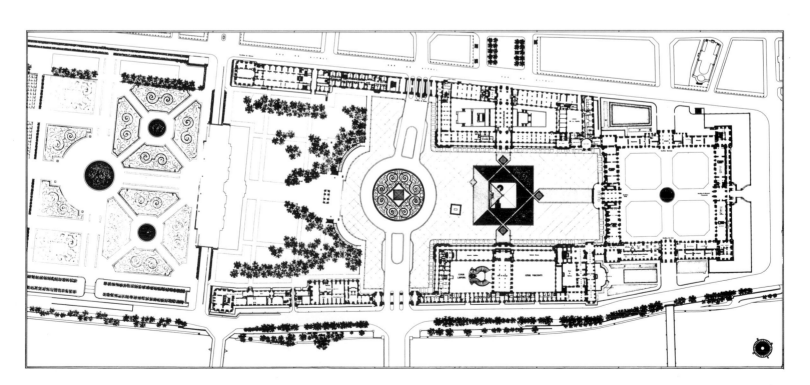

LE GRAND LOUVRE
GROUND LEVEL

The architects felt the best solution was to go underground, build connecting links under the inner court of the U-shaped complex, and construct an entrance in the middle of the plaza, the Cour Napoleon. Of course, the problem was how to design a structure that would not compete with, or detract from, the historic buildings that were begun in 1202. They chose pure geometric form as their solution—a pyramid of laminated ''white'' glass sealed with structural silicone. The structure of the pyramid is solid stainless steel, custom crafted. The solid bars were welded into place and then extended by a network of

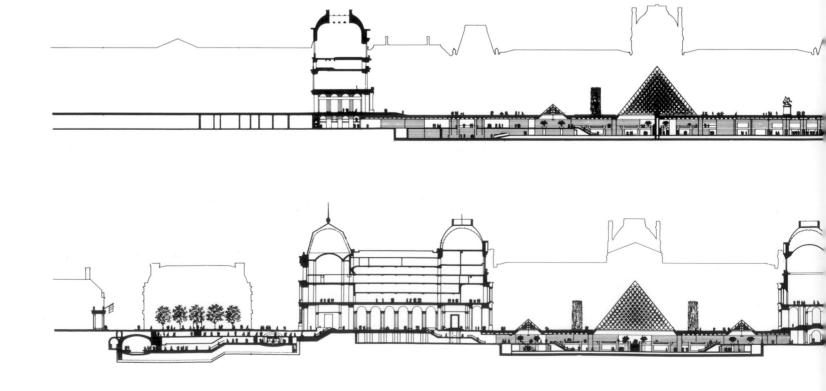

tension and compression members which use the same principles as advanced yacht racing technology. Each glass panel is set into an aluminum frame with minimal mullions, engineered to be flush with the glazed surface.

What is the consequence of this careful craftsmanship, exquisite detail in planning and advanced technology? The result is a central entry point for all museum spaces that does not detract from any of the historic value of the existing structures. Each of the pyramids (there are three smaller ones which denote interior entrances to the three wings, provide interior light and orient the visitor) defines the space and allows the existing buildings to be viewed through their transparent surfaces. The underground structure, with its cast concrete coffered ceiling and limestone walls and floors provides the

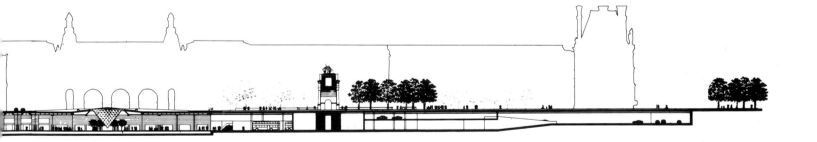

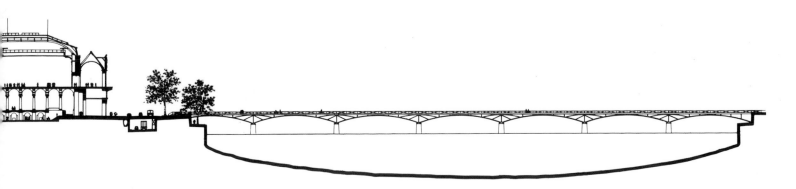

support and circulation spaces necessary for the maintenance and continuation of this great museum.

The elegance of these sparkling pyramids amid the computerized water works of the fountains adds another important architectural element to the urban scape of Paris.

PROJECT NAME:
New Glass Roof for the Inner Courtyard of the
Hamburg Museum of Local History
LOCATION:
Hamburg, Germany
CLIENT:
Verein der Freunde des Museums für
Hamburgische Geschichte e.V.
ARCHITECT:
Architekten von Gerkan, Marg + Partner; Volkwin
Marg, design
PHOTOGRAPHY:
Prof. Volkwin Marg and Bernt Federau

New Glass Roof for the Inner Courtyard of the Hamburg Museum of Local History

Hamburg, Germany

Augmenting an Original Concept

With the NEW GLASS ROOF FOR THE INNER COURTYARD OF THE HAMBURG MUSEUM OF LOCAL HISTORY, architects of von Gerkan Marg + Partner actualized what was, at the time of its inception, a concept for the museum as a whole. The museum was to be (as this innovative contemporary design solution shows) a group of buildings around an interior courtyard, protected by a glass roof. However, as in many design concepts, the idea of a glass roof was supplanted by the idea of an open space to showcase historical architectural ornamental pieces such as the Petri Portal from 1604-5.

Weathering and pollution, however—one of the penalties of technology—have taken their toll, and the original idea was seen to have merit. So the architects now were faced with the problem of either trying to construct a glass roof in the style of the original architecture (now classified as a historical monument) or designing a glass structure based on the latest in technology. They chose the latter.

The two intersecting vaults of this lightweight roof of steel-frame grid construction, statically stiffened by diagonal bracing to form a skin, are covered by "heatable, single glazing sunprotection-safety glass." The vaults, unlike their historic stone counterparts, flow into one another at their intersection in a smooth configuration that delights the senses and preserves the artifacts.

PROJECT NAME:
Nagoya City Art Museum
LOCATION:
Nagoya, Japan
CLIENT:
Nagoya City
ARCHITECT:
Kisho Kurokawa Architects & Associates
PHOTOGRAPHY:
Tomio Ohashi
AWARD:
Silver Medal at "The Fourth World Biennale of
Architecture" in Sofia, 1987—International Union
of Architects

Nagoya City Art Museum

Nagoya, Japan

A Symbiosis of Art, Architecture & Nature

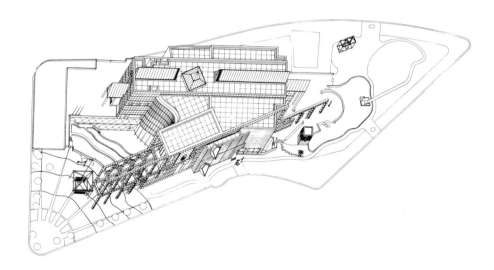

In order to allow the building to exist on the

site in a symbiosis with the natural

environment, the architects of Kisho

Kurokawa Architect & Associates designed

the NAGOYA CITY ART MUSEUM with a

portion of the exhibition space underground.

To make this "underground" area also open

to, and a part of, the site, the designers

stepped the approach to the lower level in a

series of three undulating sloped and planted

seems to produce a symbiosis between the building and the works of art displayed.

Two bridges span this two-story space, one on top of the other, allowing still more divergent views, and also efficient means of circulation between the two wings.

On the exterior, the architects have used porcelain tile and aluminum to achieve the clean, uncluttered surfaces that allow the assembled geometric forms to stand out as they intersect, butt up against and punch through each other. The three acrylic skylights not only allow natural light into the interior galleries, but they give the flat roof areas a sense of definition and play.

terraces, complete with benches at each change of level for rest, relaxation and viewing.

Through the entrance at the bottom level, one enters an enormous three-story space behind the undulating glass curtain wall that separates the museum interior from the sunken courtyard bisecting the two wings of the building. This steel and glass curtain wall with its projecting and upwardly concentrating mullions, introduces a sculptural quality into the building that

The steel and reinforced concrete structure seems alternately playful and serious as one wanders through the myriad of interior and exterior spaces, offering as many surprises as the art forms themselves.

The starkness of the building with its white marble floors, black and color used only for accents and furniture designed by the architect seems, in many ways, to be a stage set designed for the art. Perhaps this is the true function of a museum.

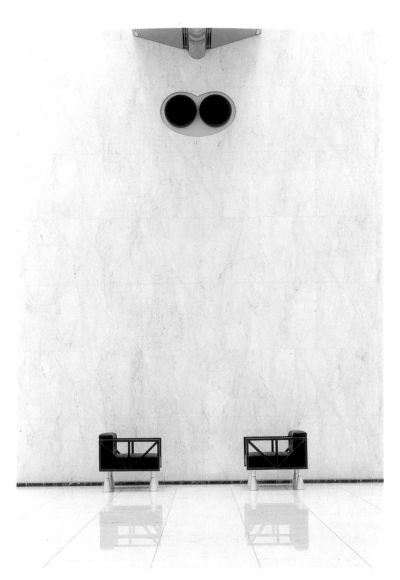

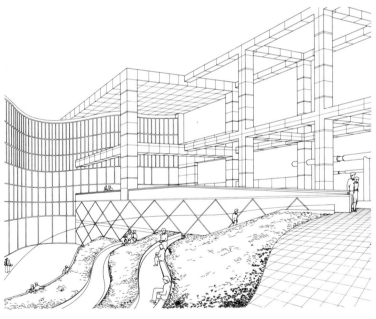

PROJECT NAME:
North Rhine Westfalia State Parliament House
LOCATION:
Düsseldorf, West Germany
CLIENT:
Land Nordrhein-Westfalia
ARCHITECT:
Eller Maier Walter, architects and engineers;
Michael Dorstelmann, project architect
PHOTOGRAPHY:
Marliese Darsow
AWARD:
Architectural Award of Germany, 1989—
Ruhrag AG

North Rhine Westfalia State Parliament House

Dusseldorf, Germany

A Circular Composition

the NORTH RHINE WESTFALIA STATE PARLIAMENT HOUSE designed by the architects of Eller Maier Walter is a study in circular spaces. This network of circles, executed in cast-in-place reinforced concrete for the walls and floor slabs, long-span steel girders for the plenary hall roof and copper, aluminum and glass for the curtain wall, is sited on the banks of the Rhine River where an active harbor once existed. Sandstone

freedom of speech. From this requirement, came the concept for the entire complex. Each circular form seemed to motivate another, and the idea was successfully carried out through the intersecting and connecting curved walls, openings, terraces and cantilevers. The forms seem to orbit around the central plenary hall in the way

cladding is carried from the outside to the inside, glass is used to give a sense of openness and accessibility. From this advantageous site, one can view the city scape of Dusseldorf and the activities on the river itself: the two hearts of the city.

The design of this structure was based on a design competition which called for a circular plenary hall. It was felt that a circular form would symbolize democracy and a sense of community despite political diversity. A circle would express a space for

satellites orbit around a sun or a central planet.

This concept and analogy is also carried out in the functional aspects of the spaces. The building opens from the center out; the approaches and entrances are from

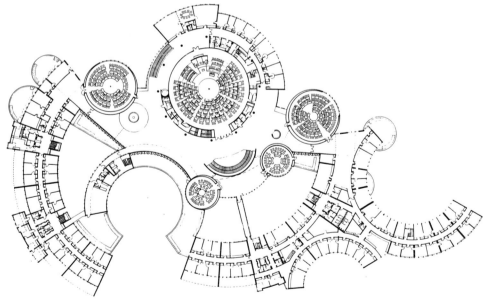

building, a building to communicate with the people, a building as transparent as the parliament ought to be.''

With the soaring, fenestrated and skylit interior spaces where politicians meet, musicians play and the public is free to observe, this structure seems to reflect the dynamic of the interweaving forces that make up the constituency.

a central court. The public is encouraged to view the parliamentary proceedings from the platform above the plenary hall. The concept is to encourage the public's perception of the openness of the government process. Fritz Eller of the design firm describes the concept and the architectural outcome this way, ''we created an inviting public

PROJECT NAME:
Australian Parliament House
LOCATION:
Canberra, Australia
CLIENT:
Parliament House Construction Authority
ARCHITECT:
Mitchell/Giurgola & Thorp Architects
PHOTOGRAPHY:
John Gollings

Australian Parliament House

Canberra, Australia

A Balanced Structure In a Natural Setting

the designers of the collaboration between Mitchell/Giurgola and Richard Thorp produced the winning design for the new AUSTRALIAN PARLIAMENT HOUSE in Canberra, Australia. Situated on a rounded hill overlooking the town, the building takes advantage of the naturally circular site and consists of a linear sequence of formal meeting rooms framed by two massive, stepped curvilinear walls, each of which

buildings. Where the spans were great, steel was used to achieve a clear span and open space. The curvilinear walls are surfaced in both polished and honed gray-pink granite and pre-cast panels. Green marble and polished black granite are used as accents on the walls, and the interiors liberally use

encloses either the Senate Chambers or the chambers of the House of Representatives. This complex is designed to separate and yet organize the various functions of government.

Cast-in-place reinforced concrete was used for the curvilinear walls as well as the majority of the construction of the other

acropolis crowned by the flag of Australia waving from the stainless steel mast that seems to grow from the form of the building, is a proud reminder of what thoughtful designers can achieve in the service of government.

marble veneers on both the horizontal and vertical surfaces.

Circulation is achieved by a series of skylight corridors between the spaces. A large skylight, actually a glass roof, is situated over the Member's Hall (the central and pivotal space in the plan) and the dark marble floor is punctured with a pool to reflect the movement and configurations of the clouds.

Each of the symmetrically arranged chambers has a different floor plan and interior configuration, further delineating the parallel but still different branches of the government. Careful study has gone into symbolism in this formal, yet organic arrangement of offices and public spaces. The public is brought in to observe the government functions, and yet the members of government have private areas to work and meditate.

Situated on top of the hill, separate, yet seen from the city, this modern day

PROJECT NAME:
Almere Town Hall
LOCATION:
Almere City, The Netherlands
CLIENT:
Municipal Almere
ARCHITECT:
Cees Dam & Partners, design—including interior
and furnishings
PHOTOGRAPHY:
Thomas Delbeck

Almere Town Hall

Almere City, The Netherlands

An Arrow & a Circle

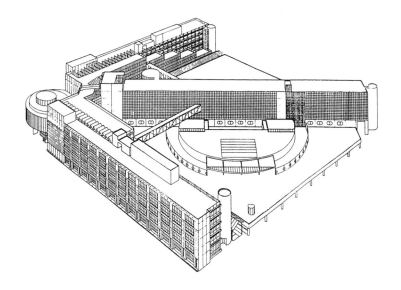

In designing the new ALMERE TOWN HALL on a site between a plaza and the banks of Weerwater, the architects of Architectenburo Cees Dam employed three wings—two at right angles and one located diagonally across the site, with a circular focal accent for the Council Chamber where the three elements intersect. This intersection point, this circular apex, becomes the circulation hub of the entire complex.

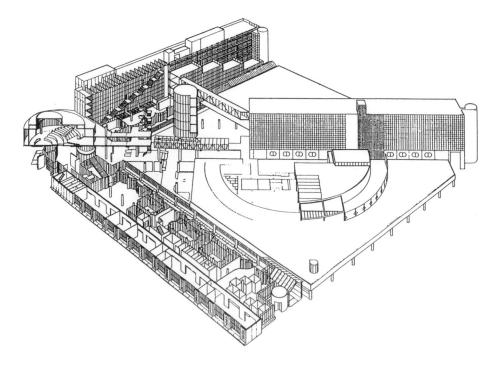

This complex of structural steel and concrete with its prefabricated aluminum framed windows, skylit roofed corridors and sawtoothed roofs is a contrast between industrial materials and timeless materials of marble, tile, gold mosaic and rosewood paneling. In fact, the contrast in materials is a definitive touch in this tour de force of contemporary design. In integrating the offices, public municipal functions, council chamber, parking, and a restaurant, the architects had to achieve a unity of design in the building, while at the same time, delineate the functions and orient the user to the various areas. Energy conservation was also an important factor.

To accomplish keeping energy consumption at the lowest possible levels, the passageways, voids in the office wings and central hall are sealed but unheated. They, in effect, are transition areas between the outside and inside. Natural ventilation is also used along with a computer-controlled energy saving system.

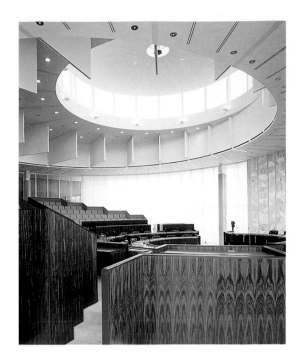

In terms of keeping the functions of the building as diverse as possible, the council chamber is designed with movable walls that open it up to the ground floor. It has a flexible seating arrangement and the acoustics are designed so that it's possible to use this space for concerts as well as chamber functions. In effect, it can function as an amphitheater.

As one studies the facade with its prefabricated panels of marble cladding and insulation attached to prefabricated concrete by stainless steel ties, and the innovative surprises of glass block inserts both horizontally and vertically, one is constantly delighted by the interplay of light, space, color and texture. The contemporary aspect of design is always in the forefront in this structure; you are definitely aware that this complex comes out of an industrial tradition. Yet, at the same time, you are aware that the designers delight in the use of humanizing elements in this massive structure. What could have been cold and intimidating has been made warm and lively through the thoughtful articulation of structural solutions to achieve workable spaces scaled and decorated to the human worker and visitor.

PROJECT NAME:
Charlotte-Mecklenburg Government Center
LOCATION:
Charlotte, North Carolina
CLIENT:
City of Charlotte, Engineering Dept.
ARCHITECT:
J.N. Pease Associates
PHOTOGRAPHY:
Gordon Schenck
AWARDS:
Honor Award (Built Project Category), 1989—AIA,
Charlotte Section; Special Recognition (Unbuilt
Project Category), 1987—AIA, Charlotte Section

Charlotte-Mecklenburg Government Center

Charlotte, North Carolina

A Civic Symbol & a Public Place

In describing the CHARLOTTE-MECKLENBURG GOVERNMENT CENTER in Charlotte, North Carolina, the words "sleek," "elegant," "clean," come to mind. In this monolithic triangular form, the architects of J.N. Pease Associates created a civic symbol that is both memorable and describable in the public's mind. By using the triangular shape and

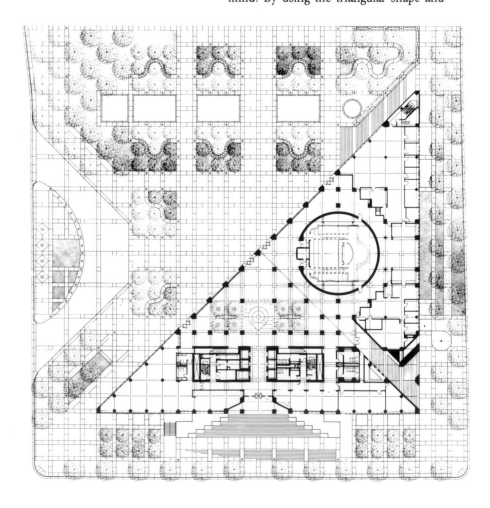

enclosing the circular Meeting Chamber

within the space, the designers also created

an interior symbolism that helps to orient

the visitor to the functions of the various

parts of government. One has only to enter

the center and view the circular form

standing across from the entry doors, to

know exactly where the meetings are taking

place.

By using a composite system of

granite panels on steel truss frames

alternating with reflective insulating glass flush mounted on four sides with structural silicone adhesive, the architects were able to design a building in which the granite was part of a curtain wall rather than a load-bearing wall. The curtain wall configuration itself is carefully studied, and incorporates a light shelf and an upper glazing band to bring light deep into the office spaces.

Another advantage the architects enjoyed, was being able to use lightweight concrete to accommodate the two floors the owners decided to add to the building after construction had already begun. This lightweight concrete mix enabled them to add the floors without redesigning and altering the foundation configuration to accommodate the additional load.

Although the designers may have chosen the triangular shape because it accommodated the zoning requirements for the building mass, the shadow patterns and the orientation of the existing buildings, the choice has produced a classical monumental structure that adds a note of timelessness to the structure.

PROJECT NAME:
Charles River Park Synagogue
LOCATION:
Boston, Massachusetts
CLIENT:
Charles River Park Synagogue
ARCHITECT:
CBT/Childs Bertman Tseckares & Casendino Inc.:
Richard Bertman FAIA, Maurice F. Childs, Charles
N. Tseckares FAIA
PHOTOGRAPHY:
Hutchins Photography
AWARDS:
Honor Award, 1974—Dept. of Housing and Urban
Development; First Honor Award, 1974—Guild for
Religious Architecture

Charles River Park Synagogue

Boston, Massachusetts

A Living Memorial

the CHARLES RIVER PARK SYNAGOGUE, designed by CBT/Childs Bertman Tseckares & Casendino Inc., was conceived as a living memorial to the original West End Jewish Community Synagogue that was razed in an urban renewal expansion in the 1950s. In the true sense of a monument, the building has a sculptural quality, is sited with space and landscaping on all four sides, and is designed to be viewed from above and below. The synagogue is situated in the middle of high-rise apartment houses built during the urban-renewal.

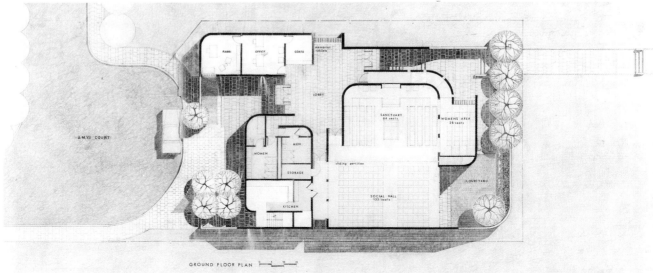

GROUND FLOOR PLAN

In order to insure privacy and yet provide light inside the sanctuary, the architects used "Kalwall," a translucent material, for the sloping ceiling. This ceiling, which slopes from 10 feet at the rear to 25 feet at the front, is supported by laminated pine beams. The exterior walls of the 5000 square foot building are faced with fluted masonry blocks both on the outside and the inside. The use of this textured surface on the interlocking screen walls allows the worshipper to enter the space feeling the timeless sense of the permanence of stone. The use of the precast unit masonry instead of stone, however, was more economical.

The lighting of the interior is accomplished by mounting fluorescent tubes on the struts, with grills beneath the tubes to soften and diffuse the light. The system also helps to define the structure by delineating the ceiling supporting structure.

Sliding glass doors open onto an enclosed courtyard that becomes a ceremonial space for weddings and other holidays when weather permits. All in all, the rebirth of a synagogue in this neighborhood has been both an architectural and spiritual triumph. Although the majority

of this building was executed with contemporary materials from the industrial age, tradition and ageless artifacts have been incorporated. The tablets over the ark are of stone from Galilee, the square shape of the synagogue is in the Talmudic tradition, and the script was patterned after the Shiloah inscription from the 8th century B.C.E.

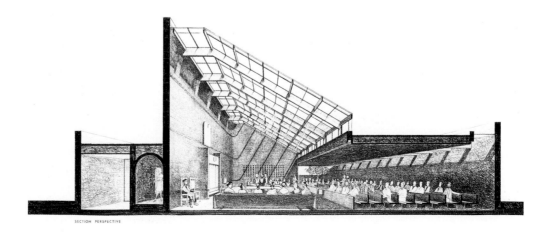

SECTION PERSPECTIVE

PROJECT NAME:
Good Shepherd Lutheran Church
LOCATION:
Fresno, California
CLIENT:
Good Shepherd Lutheran Church
ARCHITECT:
L. Gene Zellmer Associates: L. Gene Zellmer
PHOTOGRAPHY:
Wayne Thom and Alan Weber
AWARD:
Award of Merit, 1983—AIA, San Joaquin Chapter

Good Shepherd Lutheran Church

Fresno, California

Inspiration from the Nomads

In Fresno, California, L. Gene Zellmer helped the congregation of THE GOOD SHEPHERD LUTHERAN CHURCH achieve their goal of building a church that would approach expressing a religious statement, would be a spiritually moving structure in itself—and all at reasonable cost.

By using a structural fabric for the

roof, the building was completed in five months—and at a reasonable cost. It has a soaring silhouette that appears both transcendent and poised above, but not part of, the earth on which its foundations rest. In this way, perhaps it approaches expressing a religious statement.

Three glulam structural beams, anchored to the ground independently of the building, support the roof fabric, a woven fiberglass teflon coated fabric, "Sherrfill." The base of the building is a concrete slab, and conventional wood frame

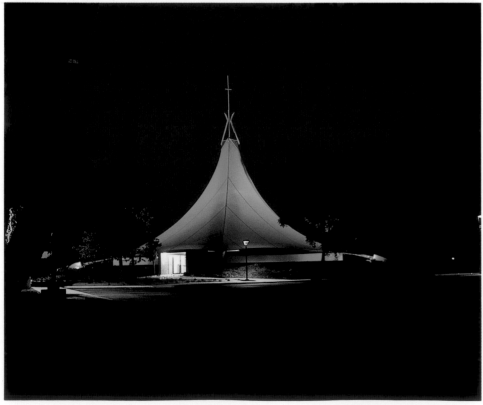

construction is used throughout the structure. The walls, however appear to float because of the mechanical panels thrust outward from the facade of the building.

The ease of construction through the selection of materials allowed this project to be completed in five months. And the sense this building projects—of a giant bird, perhaps even a dove—is well within the goal of creating a "spiritually moving structure."

PROJECT NAME:
Holy Trinity Parish Church
LOCATION:
Dublin, Ireland
CLIENT:
Rev. Joseph Collins (deceased)
ARCHITECT:
A. & D. Wejchert, Architects:
Danuta Kornaus-Wejchert, partner-in-charge;
Paul Roche, project architect
PHOTOGRAPHY:
Pieterse Davison International Ltd.
AWARD:
Highly Commended in the Parish Church
Architectural Competition, 1976—Archdiocese of
Dublin

Holy Trinity Parish Church

Dublin, Ireland

An Ambience of Calm

"The exciting shape of <u>HOLY TRINITY PARISH CHURCH</u>*, Dublin, derives from a simple square steel-frame structure comprising four RHS stanchions supporting raking roof beams. Stability is provided by a lateral steel brace at the mid-section of the roof walls and large areas of bronze reflective glass enable soft brown light to filter through and create an ambience of calm."*

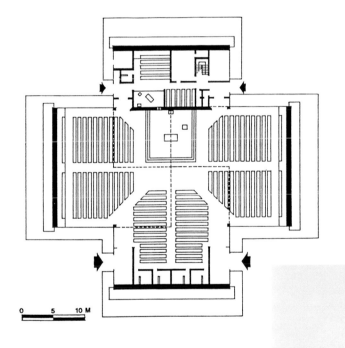

0   5   10 M

This critic's description of the award winning church by A. & D. Wejchert simplifies the original impression of this cruciform structure. Being aware mainly of the excitement of the roof structure, at first glance, the simplicity of the sloping planes, each intersecting the next, is not readily apparent. But when one studies the structure, it becomes clear that simple materials and a simple concept were used in the awe-inspiring design solution.

For example, each of these sloping roof walls is surfaced in concrete tiles to tie the building into the neighboring structures. The glazed walls of the building are Bronze Profilit cast solar control glass in standard aluminum frame supported on steel channels. Other interior walls are exposed concrete block. All are simple industrial materials that fit within the guidelines of an economical structure.

These highly technological materials have not created a sterile interior atmosphere, however. The soft warmth of the bronze light, and the symbolic triangular windows created by the structural configuration of the building express a mood of religious contemplation. The orientation of the congrégation in the cruciform plan with its central altar, no one more than 15 meters from the sanctuary to the farthest seat, creates an intimacy with religious ceremony and expression that can only help to strengthen the bonds between God and man.

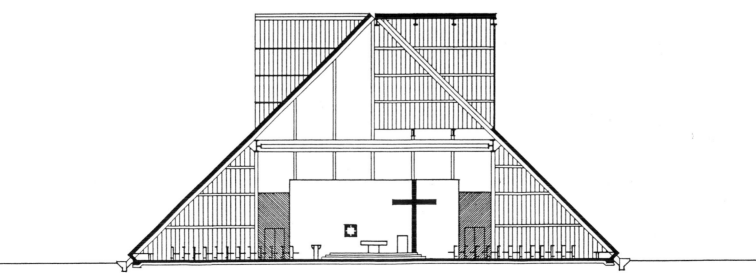

PROJECT NAME:
St. Joseph's Hospital
LOCATION:
Stockton, California
CLIENT:
St. Joseph's Hospital
ARCHITECT:
Anshen & Allan: Derek Parker AIA, princi[
charge; Bob Chan AIA, project manager; [
Borkovi AIA, project designer; Don A. Will
and Christian Oakes, project team

St. Joseph's Hospital

Stockton, California

*A Medical Mall on a
Human Scale*

In ST. JOSEPH'S HOSPITAL Stockton,

California, an expansion program will include

an outpatient surgery, a cancer center,

research laboratories, an admitting and

surgery holding area and a heliport. All

these functions (called a freestanding

outpatient treatment center) will be arranged

in a "medical mall" fashion. The architects,

Anshen + Allen of San Francisco, feel that

this concept (which necessitates building all

one-story structures) keeps the hospital on a

human scale.

The idea of human scale being a

necessity for the comfort, well being and

healing potential of the patients is a strong

focus in this addition to an existing medical

care facility. Expanding on this idea, the

architects have developed a fine arts

program that integrates works of art with

areas for art, then make sure that the structure—steel frame, waffle slab and wood-style hybrid—could accommodate the various pieces. In some cases, ceilings were lowered or raised, arches and niches were designed and backing plates designed to support the work. Lighting and landscaping were also designed around the art. In this way, rather than implementing the art after the construction was finished, the integrated works of art were able to comply with the restrictive code requirements applicable to hospital construction in the state of California.

The resulting structures with their exterior panels of Glass Fiber Reinforced Precast Concrete (GRFC), is an amalgam of architecture and art.

the architecture. The idea for this program came out of the solution to a rather mundane problem. In the lobby, they wanted to keep a window to a courtyard because it would allow natural light into the lobby. The view, however, was undesirable, so the decision was made to use a stained glass panel which would provide illumination but block the view.

Research led the architects to Reims

and the manufacturer of Marc Chagall's stained glass windows. The success of this window led the hospital to adopt the architect's recommendation of an extensive art program which, in addition to stained glass windows, encompasses wood and metal sculpture, mosaic, painting, tapestry and carved wooden doors.

To accommodate and integrate these art works the designers had to identify the

Walter C. Mackenzie Health Sciences Centre

Alberta, Canada

PROJECT NAME:
Walter C. Mackenzie Health Sciences Center
LOCATION:
Alberta, Canada
CLIENT:
University of Alberta Hospitals
ARCHITECT:
U.H.S.C. Architects Group Ltd./a joint venture of
Zeidler Roberts Partnership/Architects, Groves
Hodgson Palenstein Architects Ltd., and Wood &
Gardener Architects Ltd: Eberhard Zeidler,
partner-in-charge-of-design
PHOTOGRAPHY:
Balthazar Korab
AWARD:
Architectural Design Citation for Healthcare,
1986—Modern Healthcare and AIA

A High-Tech High-Rise Hospital

t he WALTER C. MACKENZIE HEALTH
SCIENCES CENTRE in Edmonton, Alberta,
Canada is a medical facility with more the
appearance of a resort hotel than a hospital.
The two glass gallerias not only allow
patients to look out over the landscaping
and restaurant areas, this architectural
solution also has an energy conservation
feature; it reduces the building envelope by
76 percent. The arrangement of spaces

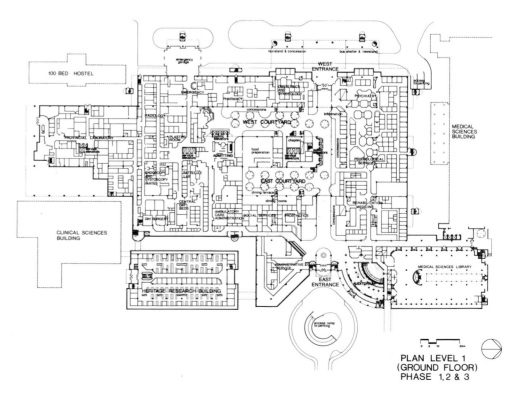

PLAN LEVEL 1
(GROUND FLOOR)
PHASE 1, 2 & 3

around the two galleries allow all patients a view. Those who don't look down on the interior space, look out over the landscape.

The architects of the <u>Zeidler Roberts Partnership</u> were concerned not only with creating an environment that would be emotionally soothing to both patients and staff, they were also charged with developing a solution that would be responsive to inevitable internal changes as medical technologies evolved, without loss of the original capital investment. To accomplish both these goals, they used a long span structural frame with eight-foot high trusses that allowed interstitial space between all floors. The mechanical systems are incorporated into these spaces.

In keeping with this technological approach, the walls are factory-built panels of interior concrete, insulation, an air space and an exterior skin of brick and concrete bands. The material handling—an essential part of the running of any medical facility —is accomplished by a type of forklift called ''Bulkveyor'' with an automated ''telelift'' for smaller items. To add to this technology, the architects also incorporated a modular fenestration system and modular

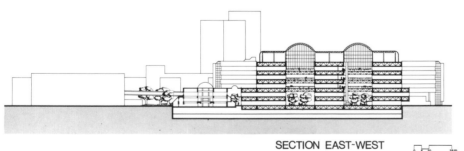

SECTION EAST-WEST

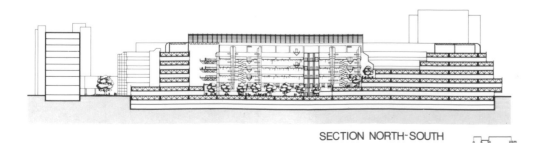

SECTION NORTH-SOUTH

polished stainless steel wall, the vermilion urethane coated steel folding screen—a traditional Japanese Byobu—with the polished black granite wall as counterpoint create an instant ambience of elegance that sets the stage for the ascent into the offices above.

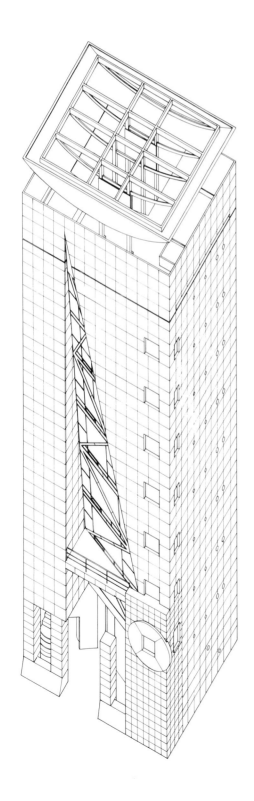

The aluminum monument which caps the building and provides it with its unique profile also serves as a source of illumination. The concept and execution of this building are, in fact, somewhat unique, and add a touch of elegance and echoes of historical form in its cap with the lilt and lift of a pagoda roof.

PROJECT NAME:
Gelco Corporate Headquarters Building
LOCATION:
Eden Prairie, Minnesota
CLIENT:
Gelco Corporation
ARCHITECTS:
The Leonard Parker Associates: Leonard S. Parker, principal-in-charge; Francis Bulbulian, project manager; Andrejs Cers, project architect
PHOTOGRAPHY:
Shin Koyama; Balthazar Korab, Ltd.; Saari & Forrai Photography
AWARDS:
Energy Conservation Award, 1976—Amarlite Anaconda Corporation; Transformation in Modern Architecture Exhibit, 1979—The Museum of Modern Art, New York; Honor Award, 1980 —MSAIA

Gelco Corporate Headquarters Building

Eden Prairie, Minnesota

Preserving the Natural Environment Through Technology

the GELCO CORPORATION required that the design of their corporate headquarters both enhance and preserve the natural environment. The site is 31 acres of forest, meadow and lakeshore in Eden Prairie, Minnesota. At the same time, however, the client needed a building designed to incorporate a highly sophisticated electronic system. The architects, The Leonard Parker Associates accomplished the client's needs to such an extent that they wrote, "At Gelco we feel particularly fortunate that we spend our working day in a beautiful, efficient facility......"

Beyond being beautiful and efficient, the reflective glass serves to integrate the mass of the building into the natural environment. The planted earth sheltered roof and wall surfaces go beyond integration into being a part of a computerized energy management system. The insulated reflective glass, heat recovery system, lighting control matrix and low consumption fluorescent lighting fixtures are also part of this total energy management system that has produced an energy consumption pattern that is 40 percent below the state energy code requirements.

Parking is screened visually on all sides by the forest, and the linking together and transition between the separate elements has been accomplished with tunnels and skyways. To create the skyway the architects used a Vierendiel truss. To achieve a transition between the ridge on which the building stands and the meadow below, the architects designed a series of giant terraced steps. And under these steps the architects located stand-by power equipment and some of the mechanical equipment. A further use by the architects of integrating the land and landscape with technology.

In terms of the interior environment, the architects were able to respond to the client's request for separate floors for each corporate department by creating the stepped configuration. And within this configuration they used an electrified cellular floor system as part of the metal deck. A raised access floor is used for the computer and tape storage rooms and a Halon fire control system is part of the total facilities design.

This unique building is a non-intrusive structure that visually seems to grow out of the landscape. It uses technology to achieve a goal, but is not governed by technology to the detriment of the landscape.

PROJECT NAME:
Union Underwear Corporate Headquarters
LOCATION:
Bowling Green, Kentucky
CLIENT:
Union Underwear Company, Inc.
ARCHITECT:
Harry Weese & Associates: Harry Weese FAIA
PHOTOGRAPHY:
Hedrich-Blessing

Union Underwear Corporate Headquarters

Bowling Green, Kentucky

Bringing the Outside Inside

the UNION UNDERWEAR CORPORATE

HEADQUARTERS was designed to fit on a

rolling site five miles outside of Bowling

Green, Kentucky. The particular site the

architects chose on this 80-acre parcel of

land was the top of a ridge, allowing vistas

over the extensive site.

Instead of attempting to make the

structure blend in, and become integral

with, the landscape, the architects—<u>Harry Weese and Associates</u>—chose to emphasize the buildings with dramatic metal mansard roofs, exposed structural systems and exterior decks punched through the roof.

These architects chose to integrate the building with the surrounding land by bringing elements of the landscape inside the building in ways that remind one of the best of Japanese architecture. In the main lobby atrium, for example, the designers have created a small garden complete with rocks, trees and a pond. Vending areas and tables are adjacent to this delightful space on one side, and offices on the others.

Other touches that emphasize the warm human scale of this building are the two-story atrium with the angular interplay of the skylights and the use of materials in general. The steel and heavy timber construction with the exposed wood joists and tongue and groove wood decking has detailing again reminiscent of Japanese architecture. The structural steel ''tree'' columns, custom designed for the building, give a sense of whimsy and delight that express the designer's control of their medium.

PROJECT NAME:
Leopardstown Business Park
LOCATION:
County Dublin, Ireland
CLIENT:
The Industrial Development Authority (IDA)
ARCHITECT:
A. & D. Wejchert: Andrzej Wejchert, partner-in-charge; Patrick Fletcher, project architect
AWARD:
An Taisce, 1989—An Taisce (National Trust of Ireland)

Leopardstown Business Park

County Dublin, Ireland

The Elegance of Pre-Fabrication

In the first buildings by the Industrial Development Authority (IDA) at LEOPARDSTOWN BUSINESS PARK in County Dublin, Ireland, the architects, A. & D. Wejchert, have used pre-fabrication in an elegant, straightforward cruciform configuration. The requirements of the IDA were for small scale rental units with a floor area of approximately 100 square

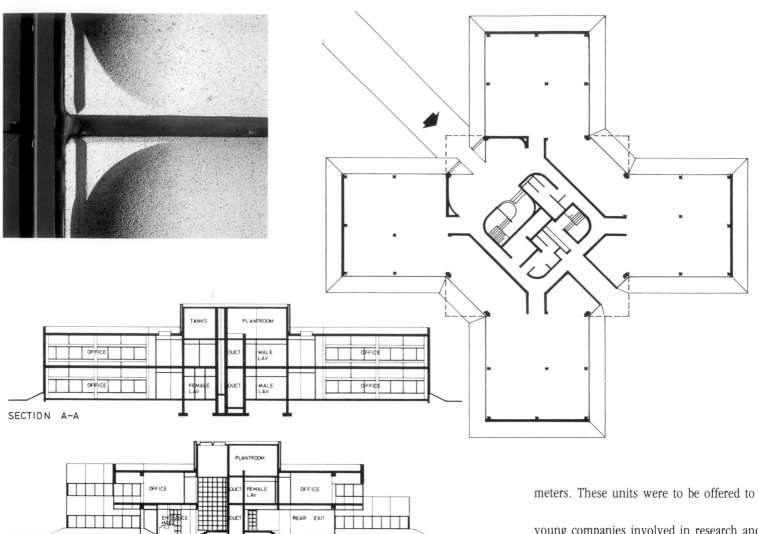

SECTION A-A

TANKS | PLANTROOM
OFFICE | DUCT | MALE LAV | OFFICE
OFFICE | FEMALE LAV | DUCT | MALE LAV | OFFICE

SECTION B-B

PLANTROOM
OFFICE | DUCT | FEMALE LAV | OFFICE
ENTRANCE HALL | DUCT | REAR EXIT

metres 0 1 2 3 4 5

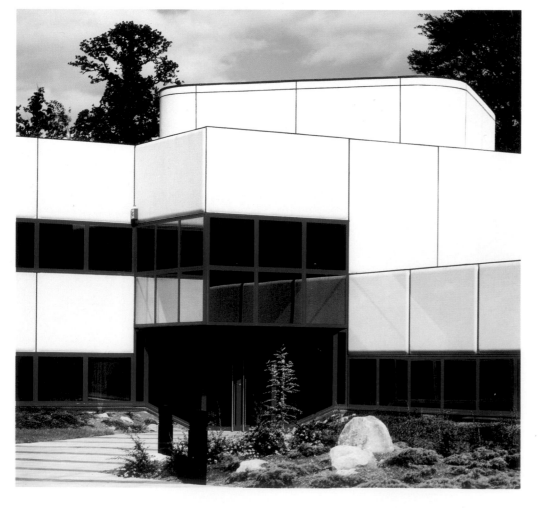

meters. These units were to be offered to young companies involved in research and development. And, like our last two examples, this building was to be situated in a mature parkland.

The use of pre-fabricated units enabled this structure to be built on a "fast track," another requirement for the project. Naturally, to create a building whose exterior elegance would match the simplicity of the plan, precision-made materials had to be employed. The architects used white glass-reinforced cement (GRC) sandwich panels, red aluminum frames and grey reflective glass. Combined with this image of "exactness and precision" is the finish of

cement and granite sand on the GRC panels. This finish is in keeping with the concept for the entire Park, which calls for the use of "stone-concrete" family of materials to echo the granite outcroppings of the area.

This building also "echoes" the surrounding environment in other ways. The grey solar glazing reflects the natural landscape and the natural elements are also brought into the interior through the use of natural ventilating and lighting. The central core contains stairways, toilets and common functions, leaving each of the four wings free for fenestration on two sides that overlook the semi-private gardens contained between the bays. These four gardens at the corners of the building are a final touch that this carefully detailed concept "allows."

PROJECT NAME:
Citicorp Center
LOCATION:
New York, New York
CLIENT:
Citybank/Citicorp (First National City Corporation)
and St. Peter's Lutheran Church of Manhattan in
the City of New York
ARCHITECT:
The Stubbins Associates, Inc.: Hugh Stubbins
FAIA, principal-in-charge/design; W. Easley
Hamner AIA, associate-in-charge; Howard E.
Goldstein AIA, project architect; Peter Woytuck,
designer
PHOTOGRAPHY:
Edward Jacoby and Norman McGrath

AWARDS:
R.S. Reynolds Memorial Award for Distinguished
Architecture using Aluminum, 1981; Honor Award
for Achievement of Excellence in Architectural
Design, 1979—AIA; Award for Excellence in
Architectural Design, 1978—Boston Society of
Architects; Albert S. Bard Award for Merit in
Architecture and Urban Design, 1978—City Club
of New York; Architectural Award for Excellence,
1978—American Institute of Steel Construction;
Certificate of Merit for Excellence in Design,
1978—New York State Association of Architects;
Outstanding Contribution to Life in New York
City, 1978—AIA New York Chapter; Award for
Design Excellence, 1977—Building Owners and
Managers

Citicorp Center

New York, New York

An Indoor Urban Plaza

the CITICORP CENTER was designed by The Stubbins Associates on a site that originally contained St. Peter's Lutheran Church. The negotiations for the property included the razing and replacement of the 1906 gothic-style structure. The result of both the negotiations and the culminating design have produced an aluminum giant rising arrogantly, cantilevering out on each corner from its four mid-span columns and nestling the new granite-clad, sky-lit, cuboid church at its base.

By elevating the building and cantilevering the corners from four 127-foot high pylons at each mid-span, the architects freed the site to accommodate both the church and a six-story terraced office and retail complex on the opposite side. The elevation of the tower also allows sunlight and a sense of space to permeate the site.

This, combined with the sunken plaza with its waterfall entrance to the subway, makes the space one of the most inviting in midtown Manhattan.

In addition, as an essential urban feature, the designers incorporated a seven-story atrium as a public space. Three levels of the atrium are retail levels and the remainder are given over to other functions.

This atrium with its planting, performing area, tables and chairs and telephones attracts people at all hours to come, purchase food from the many "take-out" establishments and enjoy the indoor urbanscape. The life of the city is enhanced, musical performances and art exhibits take place. The space becomes a location to meet, and sales increase. Everyone benefits.

To increase the comfort of all the tenants of the office space, the architects employed a new technological innovation to reduce sway. In the crown of the tower, a 400-ton concrete inertia block (tuned mass damper-TMD) has been installed for sway control. This, in concert with the cast-in-place concrete footings on bedrock and the structural steel frame with external diagonal bracing make the building structurally unique.

This complex of church, open outdoor pedestrian plaza, open indoor public atrium, retail spaces, office spaces and subway entrance combine to create a microcosm of urban life. In cities where alienation is a problem, the convenience of services on this one corner of a major city could pave the way for other designers and developers to achieve this combination of physical, esthetic and spiritual nourishing.

PROJECT NAME:
Grindelallee 100
LOCATION:
Hamburg, Germany
CLIENT:
Bauen + Wohnen
ARCHITECTS:
Von Gerkan, Marg + Partners:
Meinhard von Gerkan with Klaus Staratzke,
architects; Barbara Fleckenstein, Peter Sembritzki
and Harold Sylvester, assistants
PHOTOGRAPHY:
Heiner Leiska

Grindelallee 100

Hamburg, Germany

*An Urban Mix—Shops,
Offices & Housing*

in a wedge-shaped plot in a corner of nineteenth century Hamburg, Von Gerkan, Marg & Partners have creatively restored a site to its true place as part of the fabric of the neighborhood. GRINDELALLEE 100 is a mixed-use building with shops on the ground floor, offices on the second and third floors, and apartments on the fourth, fifth and sixth floors. The structure of the building comes out of the "modernist"

tradition with its use of load bearing

reinforced concrete frame cast in situ,

cantilevered concrete slabs and extensive use

of plated glass block for the staircase

exterior and glazed balconies—the "winter

gardens."

Some critics have compared the buildings to Adolf Loos' Villa Karma, but it is also likely that the architects attempted to pattern the proportions of fenestrations and details in keeping with the surrounding nineteenth-century buildings. It's important to note that the scale of the building is in harmony with its neighbors and the height and fenestrations are clearly thought out in ways to integrate the building with its surroundings.

The tower at the rear axis and the curved corner of the front facade topped with a circular glazed turret-like space, gives the building distinctive definition as a contemporary structure in keeping with German design tradition. By producing this structure in what might be interpreted as "transitional" style in this neighborhood, the architects have paved the way for an even more technologically-oriented building in future expansions.

PROJECT NAME:
Queen's Quay Terminal
LOCATION:
Toronto, Ontario, Canada
CLIENT:
Olympia & York Developments Ltd.
ARCHITECT:
Zeidler Roberts Partnership/Architects:
Eberhard Zeidler, partner-in-charge-of-design;
Gerald Stein, Dimitri Lutman and Jacob Astrug,
project managers and design team; Sharon Brant,
interior design
PHOTOGRAPHY:
Richard Bryant, Fiona Spalding-Smith and
Patricia Layman Bazelon
AWARDS:
Grand Award, 1984—Builder's Choice; National
Design Award, 1983—Canadian Housing Design
Council; Access Award, 1986—City of Toronto;
Award of Merit, 1984—Concrete Building Awards;
Award, 1985—Commonwealth Association of
Architects; Award, 1985—Heritage Canada
Foundation; Governor General's Medal for
Architecture, 1986—Governor-General of Canada;
Best Sales Office Over 500 Square Feet, 1983—
Members of the Institute of Residential Marketing;
Herman Mille of Canada Award for Commercial
Interiors (for Dance Theatre), 1983—Interior
Designers of Toronto; Excellence on the
Waterfront Award, 1989—The Waterfront Center;
Ontario Renews Award, 1983—Ontario
Government

Queen's Quay Terminal

Toronto, Ontario, Canada

Urban Life on the Waterfront

the QUEEN'S QUAY TERMINAL is a mixed-use building that combines retail space, restaurants, parking, a 450-seat theater, office space and condominium complex, complete with a glass-covered pool overlooking Lake Ontario. All in the old Toronto Terminal Warehouse, which was designated a building of historical and architectural importance by the Toronto Historical Board.

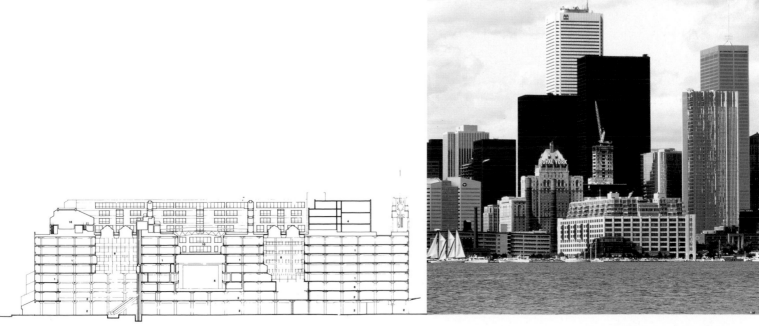

The renovation of this one million square foot unused building (completed in 1927 and considered quite modern in its day) was undertaken by the Zeidler Roberts Partnership. What they perceived as their goal was to create a new concept of urban life at the edge of the waterfront. To this end, they proceeded to make good use of the waterfront site by opening up the lower retail levels with a series of multiple entrances and opening glass doors to encourage the intermingling of pedestrian traffic from the inside and outside. The south atrium of the new configuration serves as a focal point for all the activities of the building and allows visual orientation from all areas.

To achieve this multi-use and yet not have one function impinge upon another, the architects kept the original 20' x 20' column bay layout, adding new reinforced concrete shear walls to accommodate the load of the four stories of condominiums added to the building. They also had to make structural modifications to accommodate the new stair, elevator shafts and atrium openings. Structural steel bracing members were also placed between columns to prevent buckling.

Yet, to say that the interior of this structure still has the look of the terminal it was originally built to be is not to denigrate what the architects have achieved. Rather it is to congratulate them on keeping the integrity of the historical building alive and presenting the user with spaces that recall the best of the Halles Centrales in Paris.

PROJECT NAME:
San Francisco Centre
LOCATION:
San Francisco, California
CLIENT:
The Gordon Company
ARCHITECT:
Whisler-Patri: Piero Patri FAIA, principal-in-charge;
Steve Guest AIA & Curtis Owyang AIA, project
design team; Jeff Pribyl, project manager;
Marie Zeller, planning approvals
PHOTOGRAPHY:
David Wakely / Hedrich-Blessing
AWARD:
Superior Achievement, 1990—CRAMMM; Merit,
1989—NCCA

San Francisco Centre

San Francisco, California

A Downtown Vertical Mall

n the SAN FRANCISCO CENTRE the architects of Whisler-Patri have taken the concept of a shopping mall and built vertically instead of horizontally. Using a steel moment frame structure with an exterior skin of precast concrete panels with granite facing, the designers have also created an eight-floor

structure that appears to be only four stories high. The "optical illusion," one might say was brought about by the extensive reviews by the City of San Francisco.

One of the problems that concerned the city was the impact of the sun and shadow on the surrounding area. Whisler-Patri did extensive computer-generated sun/shadow studies to determine the precise shadow impact of the new structure at key times to such areas as the cable car turn-around.

Another problem to be considered was the visual impact of the building. Since the site on Market Street had become a rather seedy area of walk-in shops, it was important to create a structure that would not only be inviting in itself, but also contribute to making the surrounding area attractive and inviting. One rationale of the building project was to attract shoppers back to the Market Street area.

A dynamic use of technology in this innovative structure—and now a major drawing card and one of its focal points—is the Mitsubishi-made elliptical, spiral escalators that take shoppers up and around the central, oval-shaped atrium. On this journey upward toward the retractable skylight, the shopper can window-shop in transit, as it were, and the shops have the advantage of passive advertising.

In its use of bronze, marble and other elegant traditional materials to present this technological solution to merchandising, the architects have not only helped the city financially, they have created a building which reminds one of the grace of the San Francisco Opera House. This new innovative structure has already inserted itself into the integral fabric of the urban landscape.

PROJECT NAME:
Eaton Centre
LOCATION:
Toronto, Ontario, Canada
CO-CLIENT:
Cadillac Fairview Corp., T. Eaton Co. Ltd.,
Toronto-Dominion Bank
ARCHITECTS:
Bregman & Hamann and Zeidler Roberts
Partnership: Eberhard Zeidler, design partner;
Sidney Bregman, co-ordinating partner
PHOTOGRAPHY:
Richard Bryant and Balthazar Korab

AWARDS:
Award of Excellence (for projects in design stage),
1974—Canadian Architect Yearbook; Certificate of
Excellence, 1978—Urban Design Awards Program;
Award of Excellence, 1981—Design Canadian;
Award, 1981—Design & Planning; Governor-
General's Award for Architecture, 1982—
Governor-General of Canada; Award of Excellence
for Large Scale Development, 1983—Urban Land
Institute

Eaton Centre

Toronto, Ontario, Canada

The Steam Ship & the Glass Cathedral

"Each building is not only a search for meaning, a look back into history and into our cultural heritage—but also a keen exploration and frugal acceptance of what we can achieve within the technology of the day. We should never be afraid of the fact that science and its technology create new forms that later may have the same emotional tension that forms of the past give us today. The dual use of technology and historic precedent

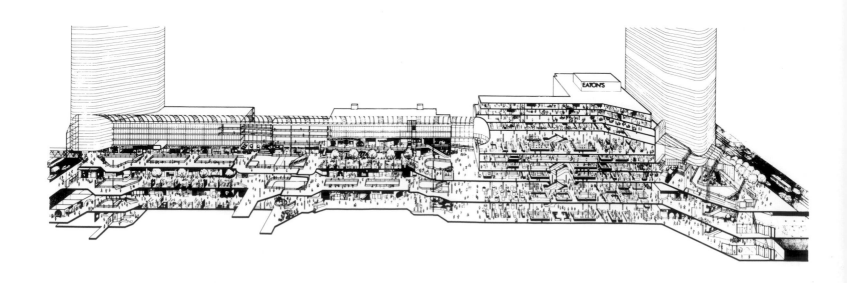

at Eaton's is perhaps the reason why the public tends to link it to two contradictory images—that of the steamship and glass cathedral. Yet many of the forms that appear primarily formal have been created out of technological exploration."

This explanation of the concept of the EATON CENTRE in Toronto by Eberhard H. Zeidler of the Zeidler Roberts Partnership expresses the approach of this design firm— integrating a new structure into the existing fabric of an urban environment, using historic precedent and new technology to achieve the overall goal. Certainly in this multi-use building (shopping mall with office towers), by using reinforced concrete, structural steel trusses, a curtain wall system for the office towers and exposed concrete, double-glazed solar and safety glass for the retail mall, they have used a myriad of contemporary materials. But beyond this, they have succeeded in integrating this structure into the immediate neighborhood.

In order to do this, the architect studied the historic precedents of the "mall," including the Galleria Vittorio Emmanuel in Milan. Their solution in many

ways visually echoes that grand space. It only echoes, it doesn't attempt to recreate. By organizing the parking and orienting each facade to the existing scale of the surrounding structures, the architects have created spaces that work, that are used —a true test of any mall—and have created a new structure with existing technology that future generations might use for a model.

The parking now is linked to the shopping levels by moving sidewalks and transparent elevators, and new technical equipment has been installed in the shops. A security system complete with a security center has been implemented. Using granite, stainless steel, interior landscaping, fountains and works of art, a new atmosphere has been created. However, the piece de resistance is the new glass roof.

This glass "umbrella" with its graceful and undulating shape was created to cover the passageways between buildings. It's supported by pillars with "tree-like" limbs

any weather—the practical aspects of this roof.

Nordwest Zentrum is now an exciting place to visit; it's attractive and people flock to it—the esthetic aspects of this roof. Who's to say which aspect is more important. Whichever it is, the center is now so successful that a hotel will open in 1991 and a multiplex cinema center in 1992.

that extend upward from the pillars supporting the garage level. These limbs support the undulating system of laminated wooden girders which support the roof. The construction of this roof was complex, and a special construction site that resembled a ship yard had to be developed. As complex and as difficult as the erection of this roof may have been, it has brought the center back to life. Shopping can now take place in

PROJECT NAME:
Conference Center and Hotel Sheraton
LOCATION:
Harare-Zimbabwe, Africa
CLIENT:
Government of Zimbabwe
ARCHITECT:
Corporation Engergoproject: Liljana and
Dragoljub Bakić, chief architects
PHOTOGRAPHY:
Bob Davey

Conference Center and Hotel Sheraton

Harare-Zimbabwe, Africa

An Exotic Tower in Africa

In Harae, Zimbabwe, Africa, Ljiljana Bakic and Dragoljub Bakic, architects from Yugoslavia designed a golden tower to express, in their words, "the hopes and beliefs of the young state of Zimbabwe." This structure, the CONFERENCE CENTER AND HOTEL SHERATON was commissioned by the Government of Zimbabwe.

The complex includes a 720-bed hotel, a cultural center that includes a "multifunctional" hall to seat 4500 and structures linking the two main buildings. The steel, aluminum and glass structure has the quality that reflects the changing light in the African landscape and stands as a beacon on the surrounding terrain. The curvilinear edges were conceived by the architects as being symbolic of understanding, friendship and cooperation between people as opposed to the sharp angular edges, which to them meant conflict.

The Zimbabwe Ruins and Victoria Falls were also cited by the architects as sources of inspiration for the softened edges of the building. Certainly in their search to design a building appropriate for a different culture and emerging nation, these designers took great pains to produce a building of

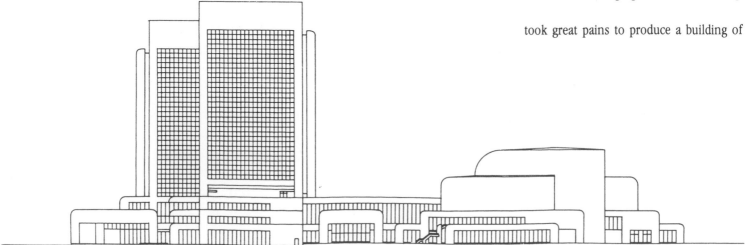

contemporary and industrial materials that would express visual ties to the past greatness of the African continent.

PROJECT NAME:
The Gallery at Harborplace
LOCATION:
Baltimore, Maryland
CLIENT:
The Rouse Company
ARCHITECT:
Zeidler Roberts Partnership/Architects:
Eberhard Zeidler, partner-in-charge-of-design;
Francis Kwok, Gerald Stein, Andrea Richardson
and Jacob Astrug, design team; Jacob Astrug,
Cliff Wildgoose and Myung Kim, project managers
PHOTOGRAPHY:
Balthazar Korab, Richard Bryant and Greg Hursley
AWARDS:
Excellence in Concrete Award (Slurry Walls), 1989
—American Concrete Institute; Award of
Excellence (Overall Concrete Structure), 1988—
American Concrete Institute

The Gallery at Harborplace

Baltimore, Maryland

A Harbor Hotel

With a diaphragm (slurry) wall as both a temporary excavation support and permanent foundation wall, ultra high-strength concrete for columns and post-tensioned concrete transfer beams, the Zeidler Roberts Partnership was able to construct their original design for THE GALLERY AT HARBORPLACE, in Baltimore, Maryland. This complex structural system— which was found to be the most economical

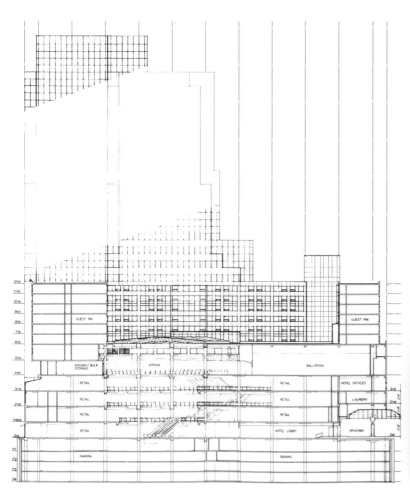

—was necessary because the site was located adjacent to Baltimore's inner harbor where the water table coexisted with the tide, except during flood conditions when the water table coexisted with the existing grade.

One might also say that the multi-use nature of the building also necessitated the study of, and use of, a highly sophisticated reinforced concrete structural system. The hotel, which occupies six levels, rests upon the atrium and a ballroom, which rests upon three retail levels, which rest upon the lobby area, which rests upon four levels of parking. An office building abuts this square structure.

The result of all this technical expertise—and careful urban studies of how the masses of the complex would affect the adjoining structures and open spaces—is an enchanting environment of fountains, skylights, planting, light and space. The exterior is faced with real granite at the base to tie it into the existing buildings, and the tower's reflecting glass and metal spandrel curtain walls are in keeping with the other tower structures of the harbor pavilion buildings.

In its essence, in its spacial surprises and play of water and multitudinous materials, it expresses the sense of an indoor Tivoli Garden.

Minneapolis Convention Center

Minneapolis, Minnesota

PROJECT NAME:
Minneapolis Convention Center
LOCATION:
Minneapolis, Minnesota
CLIENT:
City of Minneapolis
ARCHITECTS:
Minneapolis Convention Center Collaborative: The
Leonard Parker Associates, Leonard S. Parker,
design principal; Gary Mahaffey, project architect;
Setter, Leach & Lindstrom, A.J. Wilwerding,
managing principal; Loschky, Marquardt &
Nesholm, George Loschky, program principal
PHOTOGRAPHY:
Christian Korab and Phillip Prowse

Circles & Squares

by using caisson foundations, a structural steel-frame and cast-stone for the exterior, the three architectural firms known as the Minneapolis Convention Center Collaborative —Setter Leach & Lindstrom of Minneapolis, The Leonard Parker Associates of Minneapolis, and Loschky, Marquardt & Nesholm of Seattle—successfully integrated the multiple requirements for the MINNEAPOLIS CONVENTION CENTER.

The 277,000 square feet of exhibition space was designed as three separate domed exhibit halls which can also be expanded into one giant space through the use of two high-efficiency, sound-proof, retractable walls. The dome covering each of the halls is a 400-ton structural steel cap supported by four tree-like steel columns, spanning 210 feet and rising 90 feet. Each dome is copper-clad for both esthetics and function —the height allows the exhibition of boats, construction equipment and other tall items.

The entrance rotundas have skylit glass domes over the registration and pre-function lobby and provide individual entrances to allow three conventions to function simultaneously. Actually, a fourth convention could operate in one of the meeting rooms which has space for 250 exhibit booths.

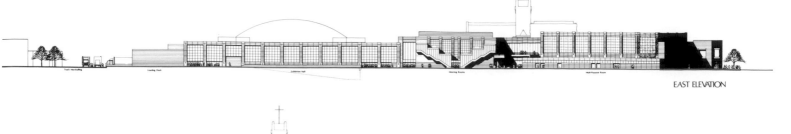

EAST ELEVATION

WEST ELEVATION

SECTION

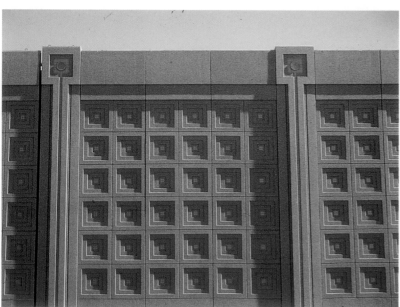

A catwalk system inside each dome allows easy display mechanisms and the utilities are accessible through 30' x 30' floor grids and overhead drops. In addition, a central computerized communications network allows direct access to the Super Computer at the University of Minnesota and a satellite link connects meeting rooms to worldwide information.

In addition to the exhibition space, the Convention Center has 87,000 square feet of meeting space, ballroom space and will be linked by skyway to hotels, shopping, the Walker Art Museum/Guthrie Theatre

Complex and other essential elements of Downtown Minneapolis. The links that the Convention Center supplies to the city of Minneapolis, however, are just beginning to be understood as this technologically advanced center attracts visitors and exhibitors from around the globe.

PROJECT NAME:
NMB Bank
LOCATION:
Amsterdam, The Netherlands
ARCHITECT:
Architectenbureau Alberts & Van Huut in cooperation with Billing Peters Ruff and Theo Crosby, Pentagram Design Ltd.
PHOTOGRAPHY:
Sybolt Voeten

NMB Bank

Amsterdam, The Netherlands

On a Human Scale

In the NMB BANK HEAD OFFICE, A. Alberts Architects have created a cluster of modular buildings, designed in an organic style that actually consumes less energy than any existing building today. This is no accident. Working together with a building physicist,

W.M. Treffers, and a building co-ordinator for the bank, the design of this complex was a synthesis of the expertise of the three participants. No one person was totally responsible for the design. There were certain criteria, of course, that influenced the design process. The bank wanted space for small separate groups to work, the

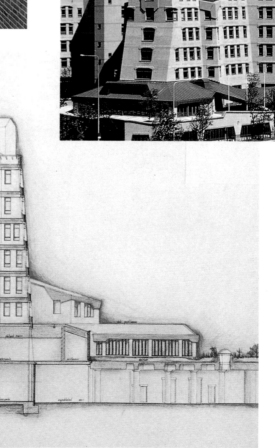

The interiors show the care the design team has taken in color and form to integrate the "organic" concept throughout

the structure. Even if one does immediately think of Gaudi, on reflection, one also thinks of Dutch heritage. The team, and especially the architect, have taken the best of current knowledge on work environments and combined it with a sensitivity to form and history that creates a series of timeless and unique architectural spaces that are designed on a human scale.

PROJECT NAME:
Lloyd's of London
LOCATION:
London, England
CLIENT:
Lloyd's
ARCHITECT:
Richard Rogers Partnership, Ltd.: Richard Rogers,
John Young, Marco Goldschmied and
Mike Davies, project directors; Richard Marzec,
project administrator; Ove Arup & Partners,
structural and service engineers
AWARDS:
Civic Trust Award, 1987; Financial Times
Architecture at Work Award, 1987; Eternit 8th
International Prize for Architecture, Special
Mention, 1988; RIBA Regional Award, 1988; PA
Awards for Innovation in Building Design and
Construction, 1988; RIBA UK Award, 1988

Lloyd's of London

London, England

Designing for Change

n designing <u>LLOYD'S OF LONDON,</u> the centre

of world insurance since the seventeenth

century, the <u>Richard Rogers Partnership</u>

decided to design for the needs of the

twenty-first century. They expressed the

overall concept in these words,

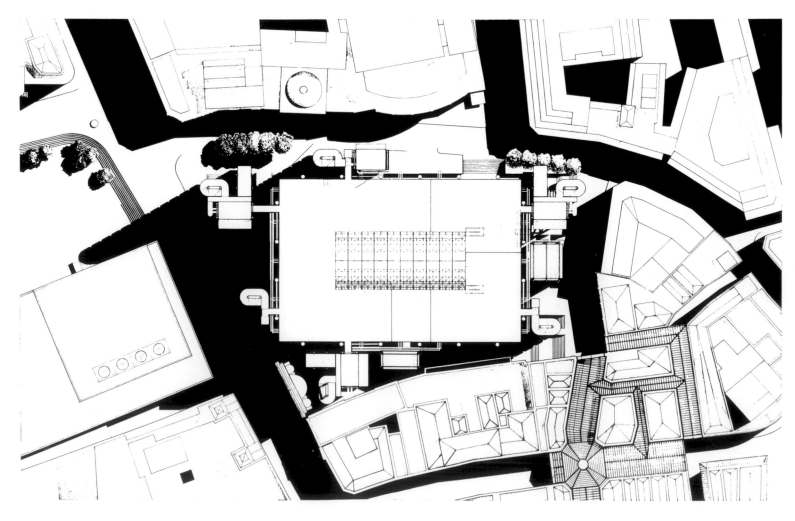

"The building is designed as a series of 16m wide concentric galleries overlooking a central atrium. Each gallery may be used either as part of the underwriting Room or as optimum office space. All normal fixed obstructions, i.e., toilets, stairs, entrances, lifts and columns are

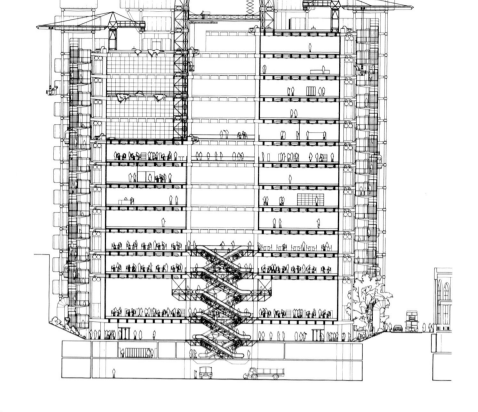

placed outside the building in six vertical towers."

This concept of placing all potentially obsolete functions on the exterior of the building, allows the areas to be easily remodeled without disturbing the integrity of the basic structure. A novel and forward-looking approach in a structure for a very traditional firm. The building materials themselves—reinforced and pre-cast concrete, steel framework, triple-layered solar control glass (incorporating part of the ventilating system), and stainless steel sandwich panels for cladding the service towers—are what one might say are "traditional technology," but the way in which these materials are combined and configured clearly speaks of the twenty-first century.

At the same time that this innovative structure shouts of the future, it pays careful attention to the past—the existing historic buildings—by stepping down the 12-story building to 6 stories on the South to keep the building in the scale of the neighborhood. The resulting terraces also provide planting and outdoor areas on the upper levels.

This shining center, this marketplace for the new century, hints of rockets to the farthest corners of the galaxy and reminds us that in technology, as in all innovative progress, nothing is static and all inventions should make way for the future.

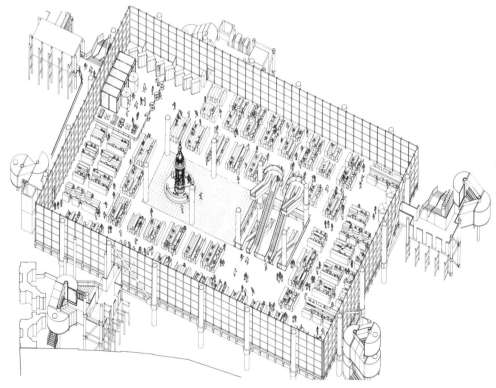

PROJECT NAME:
Fukuoka Seaside Momochi
LOCATION:
Fukuoka City, Japan
ARCHITECT:
Kisho Kurokawa Architects & Associates

Fukuoka Seaside Momochi

Fukuoka City, Japan

From Reclaimed Land in the Hakata Bay

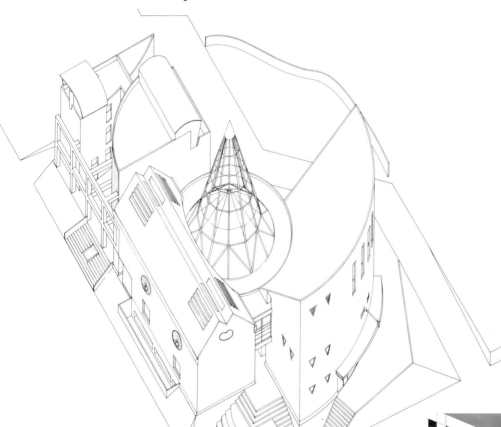

the FUKUOKA SEASIDE MOMOCHI is part of a project planned on reclaimed land in the Hakata Bay. This building, designed by Kisho Kurokawa, Architect & Associates, has been designed to function as both a bank and a commercial space. This building also serves as a pavilion in the Fukuoka Seaside Momochi Housing and Environmental Exhibition.

This exhibition features buildings designed by both foreign and domestic architects—Kisho Kurokawa, Stanley Tigerman, Hiroshi Izue, Junji Mikawa, Yasuhumi Kijima, Michael Graves, Syouei You—and is intended to present both the architecture and the town as appealing, inviting and possibly a future home either commercially or residentially.

The bank portion of this assemblage of forms has a symbolic wood-framed 23m high conical atrium in the center. Surrounding this atrium are a business room and tenant space on the second floor. The

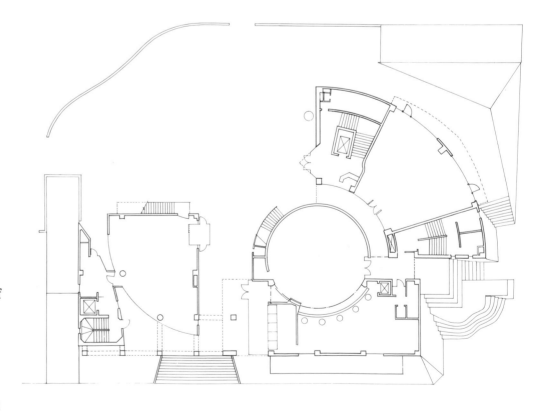

reinforced concrete walls and slabs, surmounted by the wooden truss in the hall and the grille-like motif in the glazed walls and doors, give this building a sense of its historical and cultural heritage. The eaves, window frames and staircases use aluminum and stainless steel, and many of these materials are coated with bright vermilion—traditionally Japanese.

The site hugs the edge of the sea beyond battered retaining walls and platforms of traditional stone that are reminiscent of ancient Japanese buildings. In a new town, of course, banking is essential; banking is one of the oldest institutions. So, the integration of technology and tradition in this building on new land perhaps is symbolic of the need of the new to remain linked to the past.

PROJECT NAME:
Industrial Technology Institute
LOCATION:
Ann Arbor, Michigan
CLIENT:
George H. Kuper
ARCHITECT:
William Kessler & Associates, Inc.:
William Kessler, principal designer; Todd Young
and John Milliacca, designers; Donald Osgood,
project architect; Carolyn Cardoza and
Kimberly Field, interior design
PHOTOGRAPHY:
Balthazar Korab, Ltd.

AWARDS:
Honor Award, 1987—Michigan Society of
Architects; Outstanding Achievement Award, 1987
—Engineering Society of Detroit Construction;
Construction Showcase Award, 1987—Association
of Michigan, Detroit Chapter; Honor Award, 1987
—AIA; Architectural Award of Excellence, 1987—
American Institute of Steel Construction

Industrial Technology Institute

Ann Arbor, Michigan

Machine-Made Materials

at the bottom of a topographical bowl, on a wooded site with wild grasses and a meandering stream, floating above the ground and cantilevered out over concrete columns, a sleek, horizontal stainless steel structure appears as a space station come to earth to rest briefly before once again departing for the heavens. The effect is, in

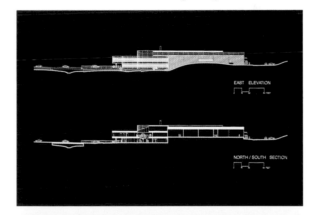

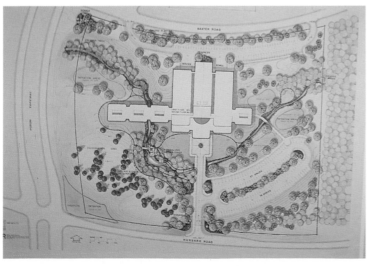

large part, deliberate.

The architects of William Kessler and Associates designed this 21st Century structure—the INDUSTRIAL TECHNOLOGY INSTITUTE—both to express the type of research the participants are engaged in (the application and design of robotics and computerized industrial systems) and to reflect, as William Kessler states, "machine-made products and materials rather than hand-crafted natural products." Using stainless steel and glass for the facade, and steel framing and concrete for the structure, this low building nestled into the natural landscape seems the perfect expression.

The "pod" arrangement of the facility with the long pods behind the atrium entrance used for the laboratory facilities and the small square "pods" on either side of the central building used for offices, also seem to speak of space technology. The rounded corners further emphasize this fantasy.

But, "fantasy" is the wrong concept for this building. Everything has been designed to be highly functional as well as elegant and futuristic. In the high-bay lab proper, the floor is an uninterrupted surface

of continuously-poured plastic-reinforced concrete which is surfaced with a rubberized coating. This allows the robot carts (which are very sensitive to joints and bumps) to have smooth access across the surface. The wall of this lab is butt-glazed along the corridor to allow the engineers to watch the robots at work, either for technical observation or for entertainment.

The interiors also express a twenty-first century concept, with burnished reflective mechanical/electrical ceiling spines and sprinkler disk heads in the dining room and high skylit corridors between "interpodal spaces." Many of these surfaces which are highly reflective, allow the

natural environment outside to be reflected inside, giving a warmer and more humane aspect to the highly technological materials.

These materials, however, contribute to the overall safety of the inhabitants of the building. For example, the fire suppression system is architecturally integrated and in place of knobs you have wires, while the sprinkler heads have been integrated into the design of stainless steel ceiling panels.

In the hovering structure with the insulated gray glass and stainless steel curtain wall with futuristic rounded corners, the architects have succeeded in telegraphing the building's functional qualities. But, when one studies the design carefully, it also becomes apparent that the architects carefully sculpted both the inside and the outside landscape to provide areas to rest, contemplate, meet and exchange ideas—the best of environments for creative research and discovery.

PROJECT NAME:
HCA Data Center
LOCATION:
Nashville, Tennessee
CLIENT:
Hospital Corporation of America
ARCHITECTS:
Gresham, Smith and Partners: Paul Plummer AIA,
principal; Steve Johnson AIA, designer;
Tom Carnell AIA, project manager
AWARD:
Design Award, 1987—AIA, Gulf State Chapter

HCA Data Center

Nashville, Tennessee

Another Kind of Automation

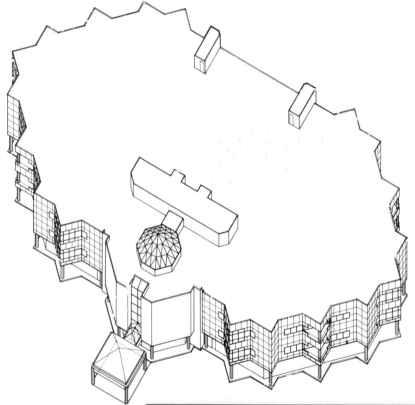

It's interesting to speculate that perhaps data processing is a new form of industrial automation. In many ways, it involves the same rote, routine functions—entering line after line of data, for example. Granted, there are also extremely complex operations combined with these sometimes rote activities, but the computer age has given birth to a new kind of production—both of the hardware and through the software.

In the HCA DATA CENTER, in Nashville, Tennessee, designed by Gresham Smith and Partners, for the Hospital Corporation of America, some of these aspects of automation were taken into account and the design adjusted accordingly. There were also other elements to be considered, however, from the client's point of view. In fact, the following client's charge to the architect will show how the program for this building touched on every aspect of the design. It includes:

- The computer room must be the central organizing element.

- The first level must have no fenestration.

- The building must present a solid and secure image to both visitors and viewers.

- The exterior must be white marble in keeping with the other buildings in the corporate campus master plan.

- State-of-the-art security systems must be incorporated.

The finished building incorporates all these aspects, but also provides a humane and esthetic setting within which to work. For example, the atrium is functional in that it allows surveillance of access to the upper floors, and it also allows natural light into the interior. And the power sources for the centrally-located computer, two electrical utility sources plus a 24-hour generator back-up, surround the central computer

hardware and computer control areas. These power sources, in turn, are surrounded and protected by the support and research/data processing areas. At the periphery of the building (the least secure space), the designers have situated the public/work areas with access to both daylight and outside balconies.

To facilitate cladding the outside in the necessary white marble, a system of mounting the white marble with the granite accent pieces onto a precast panel was used. Further advanced technology was employed in the fiber optic installations in the state-of-art security systems. In fact, this building has been described (to use Piero Patri's terminology) as not just an intelligent building, but a "very" intelligent building.

Perhaps that might account for why, with its web-like floor plan and hovering, horizontal presence, this structure seems almost sentient, as though the electronic intelligence within the structure has given it life.

PROJECT NAME:
Telecommunications Tower
LOCATION:
Lawrence, Kansas
CLIENT:
Southwestern Bell
ARCHITECT:
Gould Evans Architects, P.A.: David C. Evans,
principal-in-charge
PHOTOGRAPHY:
Hobart Jackson
AWARD:
Honor Award for Excellence in Architecture,
1980—AIA, Kansas City Chapter

Southwestern Bell Telecommunications Tower

Lawrence, Kansas

A Sculptural Landmark

the TELECOMMUNICATIONS TOWER designed by Gould Evans Architects has been praised by an architectural jury as not "just an industrial tower. It's a landmark......"

To achieve this distinction, and win an award for this unusual technologically functional architectural element, the architects studied the historic examples and symbolism of the "tower." Feeling that the

concept of the tower in history would help them arrive at a solution, they next studied the landscape and buildings within which this tower was to be erected. Scale, texture and cladding materials became important elements.

Although this structure is technological in function, and the scale is massive in comparison with the two- and three-story buildings of this Kansas town, the materials of this 156' high structure and the way in which the architects have articulated each of the four sides in a different way, delight the eye and provide the tower with the ambiance of campanile. Instead of bells, this tower has microwave equipment.

Using a high-tension galvanized steel frame with sand-formed brick cladding to echo the traditional materials of downtown Lawrence, the architects have created a landmark in the truest sense. Seen across the flat prairie, this beacon is a symbol of the sensitivity of the designer to the inhabitants of the design environment.

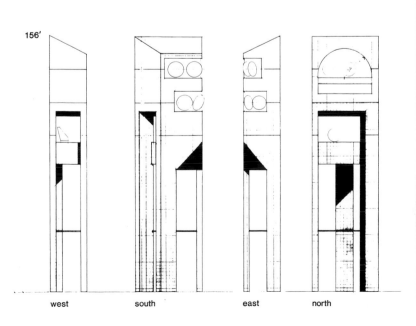

west   south   east   north

PROJECT NAME:
Albany County Airport Passenger Terminal
LOCATION:
Colonie, New York
CLIENT:
County of Albany
ARCHITECT:
Einhorn Yaffee Prescott, Architecture and
Engineering, P.C.: Steven L. Einhorn, principal-in-
charge; Eric C. Yaffee, project manager;
Timothy Cohan, project architect; James
McKinney, project designer
PHOTOGRAPHY:
Norman McGrath
AWARDS:
Passive Solar Technology, 1982—American Solar
Energy Society; Owens Corning Fiberglas Energy
Conservation, 1982—Owens Corning

Albany County Airport Passenger Terminal

Colonie, New York

The Legacy of Leonardo

Without the Industrial Revolution there would be no need for airports—Leonardo DaVinci notwithstanding. The ALBANY COUNTY AIRPORT PASSENGER TERMINAL by Einhorn Yaffee Prescott, however, does much more than just serve as a passenger terminal. The building is an excellent example of the use of solar energy in a commercial context. This terminal has been designed to use passive solar heating and natural lighting as

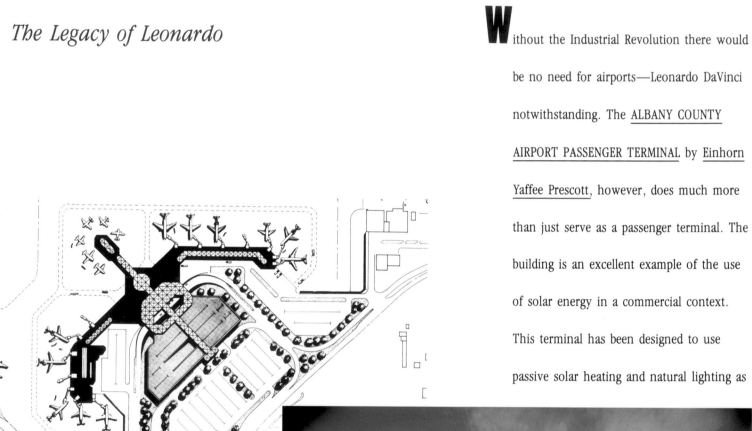

an integral feature of the design, thus conserving and generating energy. At the same time, the finished building is an exciting play in contrasts, with the heavy masonry for thermal masses playing counterpoint to the lightness of the louver and glass areas. Technology has succeeded in becoming esthetic.

Beyond the technology of solar power, the architects of this building also made use of computer technology in the design and control of the louvers. A microcomputer—a custom combination of an Apple II computer and sensory hardware—is programmed with the solar altitude and azimuth angles until the year 2000. The computer continuously

gauges the indoor and outdoor environment and adjusts the louver to the most energy-efficient position. This added feature means that with computer technology, solar power is increased in efficiency.

If you stop to consider how this technology might be adapted to the housing market—for example high-rise housing with solar panels on the roof top—the possibilities for economical energy

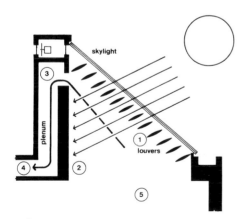

1. The operable louvers are open to allow sunlight into the building.

2. The sunlight warms a brick wall at the back of the skylight.

3. Air is drawn through a plenum behind the wall, and is heated during its passage over the warm bricks.

4. The heated air is drawn into the building heating system for distribution.

5. Natural light is provided to the space below.

Sunny Winter Day

The sun is used to provide heat and light.

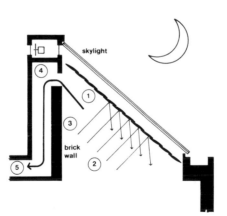

1. The operable louvers are closed to provide an insulated "ceiling" below the glass and reduce heat loss through the skylight.

2. The louvers are insulated, blocking the flow of heat from the building.

3. The brick wall remains warm for some time after sunset due to its "thermal mass".

4. Air is drawn through a plenum behind the wall, and is heated during its passage over the warm bricks. When the heat stored in the brick wall is used up, air flow through the plenum is stopped.

5. The heated air is drawn into the building heating system for distribution.

Winter Night

Loss of heat through the skylight is reduced.

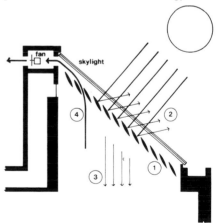

1. The operable louvers are partially open.

2. Direct sunlight is reflected by the louvers.

3. Diffuse northern light is provided to the spaces below.

4. The area below the skylight serves as a heat banking space. Warm air from the building below will collect beneath the skylight. Exhaust fans will then discharge the warm air from the building.

Sunny Summer Day

The sun is used to provide light, but is not allowed to penetrate into the building and generate excessive heat.

consumption are endless. Or perhaps there's a future solution with single family houses and personal computers. Technology is always an evolving and expanding science. When one invention or innovation is used on one building type, this breakthrough is presented to other designers who can take it the next step into a further generation of technological development.

PROJECT NAME:
Airport Berlin-Tegel
LOCATION:
Berlin, Germany
CLIENT:
Berliner Flüghafen GmbH
ARCHITECT:
von Gerkan, Marg + Partner:
Meinhard von Gerkan

Airport Berlin-Tegel

Berlin, Germany

An Urban Solution

the AIRPORT BERLIN-TEGEL, designed by von Gerkan-Marg + Partner, is, in actuality, a complex of passenger terminal building, power plant, maintenance buildings, cargo terminal, catering building, fire station, fuel station, hangars and other support structures. Designing this futuristic complex with continuous expansion in mind, the

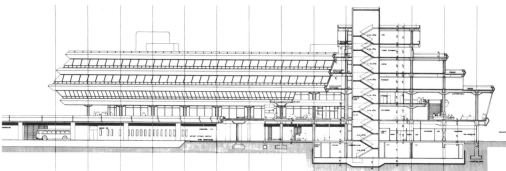

architects developed a modular concept that employed exterior cladding of aluminum panels on the differing structural systems needed for the different buildings.

They chose aluminum as the exterior skin of these structures because it was, in their words, the "same material as aircraft and passenger-loading bridges, (and had) advantages to steel sheet or plastic facades: non-corrosive, weather resistant, not inflammable, technical process of shaping, price." Perhaps some of the same reasons that aircraft designers use aluminum. Whatever the reasons, the result is successful both visually and functionally; functionality was a key concern of the architects.

Starting with a hexagonally-shaped master terminal, then adding ancillary buildings as counterpoint to this central mass, they began to work on a module that would work for all structures. They arrived at units six meters long, laid out one and one half meters from its neighbor, giving a basic grid of seven and one half meters. The vertical dimension is based on three meter module. Each building is constructed on this module and the siting would allow,

in theory, all the buildings to link up as they expand.

The designers used cast-in-place concrete for the passenger terminal and catering building, precast and prestressed concrete for the cargo terminal and a steel structure for the power plant, maintenance buildings and hangar. Differing versions of HVAC systems were also used for each structure. Concrete, enameled metal panels, carpet and brick flooring were some of the materials used on the interiors.

The interior parking in the hexagonal passenger terminal is not only a convenience for travelers, it eliminates the massive parking lot common to so many airports. This thoughtful aspect of design is only one of the ways in which the

designers have carefully thought through and articulated their design solution to this complex problem. Looking something like what one might imagine as a colony built on a far-off asteroid, this complex has about it the care, attention to detail and durability of materials of a structure designed by space scientists.

PROJECT NAME:
Canada Place
LOCATION:
Vancouver, Canada
CLIENT:
Canada Harbour Place Corporation
ARCHITECT:
Zeidler Roberts Partnership/Architects;
Musson Cattell & Partners Architects;
Down/Archambault Architects II: Eberhard Zeidler,
partner-in-charge-of-design; Alan Munn, project
architect
PHOTOGRAPHY:
Timothy Hursley

AWARDS:
Achievement Award, 1986—Downtown
Vancouver Association; Achievement Award,
1986—International Downtown Association;
Excellence on the Waterfront Award, 1988—
Waterfront Centre

Canada Place

Vancouver, Canada

A Dockside Terminal

the allusion to, and expression of, nautical elements was a conscious design decision in CANADA PLACE, a joint venture by the Zeidler Roberts Partnership, Musson Cattell & Partners and Down/Archmabault. In this complex that incorporates a Cruiseship

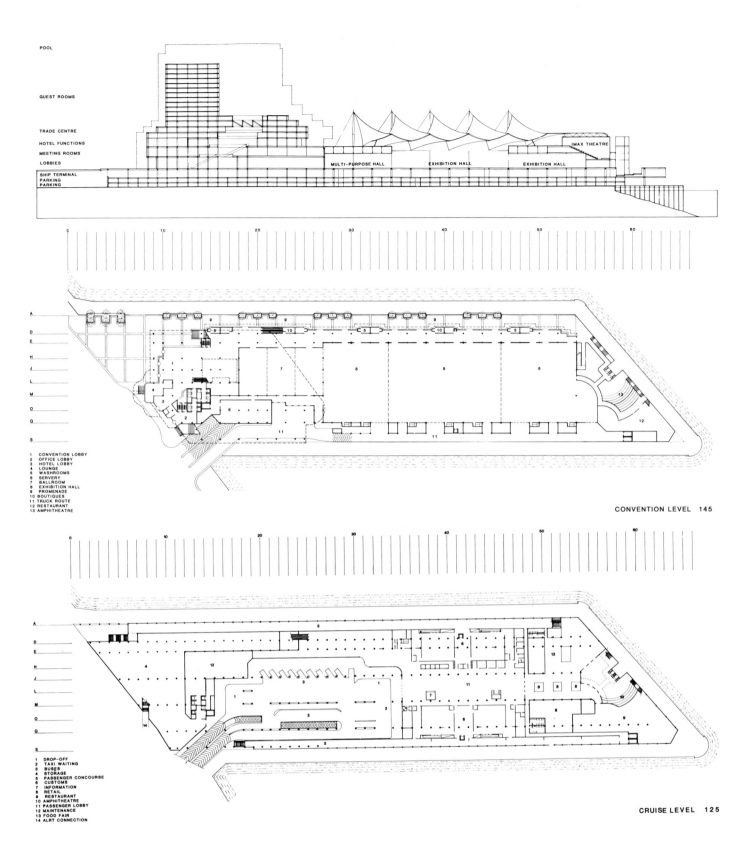

POOL

GUEST ROOMS

TRADE CENTRE
HOTEL FUNCTIONS
MEETING ROOMS
LOBBIES

SHIP TERMINAL
PARKING
PARKING

MULTI-PURPOSE HALL EXHIBITION HALL EXHIBITION HALL IMAX THEATRE

1 CONVENTION LOBBY
2 OFFICE LOBBY
3 HOTEL LOBBY
4 LOUNGE
5 WASHROOMS
6 SERVERY
7 BALLROOM
8 EXHIBITION HALL
9 PROMENADE
10 BOUTIQUES
11 TRUCK ROUTE
12 RESTAURANT
13 AMPHITHEATRE

CONVENTION LEVEL 145

1 DROP-OFF
2 TAXI WAITING
3 BUSES
4 STORAGE
5 PASSENGER CONCOURSE
6 CUSTOMS
7 INFORMATION
8 RETAIL
9 RESTAURANT
10 AMPHITHEATRE
11 PASSENGER LOBBY
12 MAINTENANCE
13 FOOD FAIR
14 ALRT CONNECTION

CRUISE LEVEL 125

Terminal, a shopping mall, an office building complex, a World Trade Centre and a 505-room hotel, the designers have created almost a miniature city at the end of what originally was a decaying 1100-foot pier at the foot of Vancouver's central business district.

In designing the Cruiseship Terminal (which can accommodate five ships simultaneously) the architects had to combat the problem of foundations on the seabed which had a limited load-carrying capacity. They solved this problem through use of a series of caissons and pile clusters and an

all-steel structure incorporating large expansion joints for earthquake loads.

The design of the sail-like teflon-coated fiber fabric roof also created problems in spanning the space with the limitations inherent in the material. By skewing the roof 45 degrees to create spans between suspension cables, the architects created this elegant roof form that produces a vault-like space over the exhibit hall. As temperature, snow and wind loads cause movement in the cable structure, it must appear that the structure is truly a ship at sea.

The aluminum and glass of the exterior walls, the railings, the promenades and the differing levels for viewing, all give the visitor the sense of viewing the arriving and departing ships from a ship. There's a sense of playfulness. One can hear the bands playing simply from the visual impact of this complex of buildings. Add to that the utilization of an abandoned area of the urban scape and you have a highly successful venture.

PROJECT NAME:
Washington Union Station
LOCATION:
Washington, D.C.
CLIENT:
Union Station Redevelopment Corporation
ARCHITECTS:
Harry Weese & Associates (restoration):
Harry Weese FAIA; Stanley N. Allan, principal-in-charge; Norman Zimmerman, designer;
Karl Landesz, project manager/project architect;
Union Station Venture Ltd. (USVL) (for new development side) comprised of: Equity Association Inc.; LaSalle Partners Ltd., Chicago; Williams Jackson Ewing Inc., Baltimore; & Benjamin Thompson & Associates Inc., Boston
PHOTOGRAPHY:
Carol Highsmith

AWARDS:
Honor Award, 1989—National Trust for Historic Preservation; Reconstruction Project Award, 1989 —Building Design and Construction; The 10th Annual Renovation Award, 1989—Commercial Renovation; Distinguished Restoration Award, 1989—AIA Chicago Chapter; Merit Award, 1989— AIA Washington, D.C. Chapter; ''A Careful Restoration of the Beaux Arts Architecture'' First Design, 1989—Mayor Barry's Environmental Design Award

Washington Union Station

Washington, D.C.

Trains, Shoppers, Diners & Movie-goers

In the renovations and revitalization of

Daniel H. Burnham's 1907 Beaux Arts

UNION STATION in Washington, D.C., the

architects of Harry Weese & Associates and

Benjamin Thompson & Associates have

created a vital vibrant space that combines

the excitement of the arrival and departure

of travel with the glamour of an elegant and

well appointed indoor shopping mall.

Complete with lower level connections to

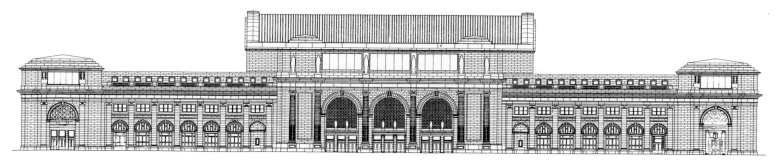

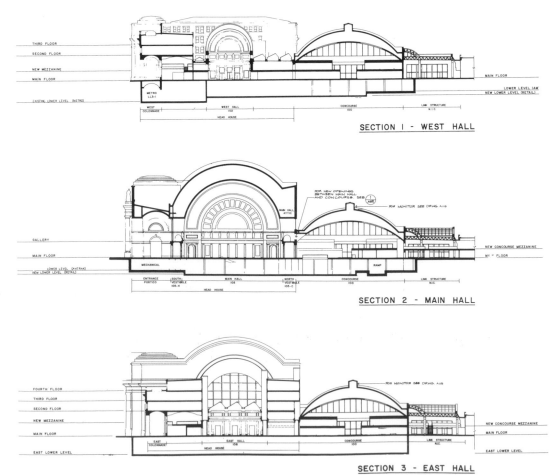

SECTION 1 - WEST HALL

SECTION 2 - MAIN HALL

SECTION 3 - EAST HALL

the underground Metro system—and a food court and a nine-screen cinema complex all installed in the basement.

To accommodate the facilities in the basement, an enhancement, the floor had to be lowered five feet below the concourse floor and nine feet below the head house floor. This was accomplished by enclosing cast-iron columns in reinforced concrete and installing a cantilevered system of beams so that columns could be aligned to provide clear sight lines in the theaters. To counteract the vibration from the subways, the theaters are isolated by floating a

reinforced concrete slab on 2 x 2 foot grid of

1 ¼ '' thick neoprene pads covered with

plywood and sheet cork.

New mechanical systems and elevators

were concealed in newly-found cavities in

the structural system and some ceiling

coffers were perforated and connected to flexible ductwork and a blower to force air to the floor. Lighting the renovated space was accomplished by attaching 4'' high high-density lighting fixtures to the tops of the columns. Restoring the finishes was another matter, however.

Using microscopes and chemical analysis, the architects of Harry Weese & Associates studied the salvaged paint samples and succeeded in duplicating the original colors and finishes. The scagliola (a technique to imitate marble) on the columns in the East Hall has been repaired or

replaced; murals and decorative stenciling has been replicated and the original marble floors have been re-installed.

Essentially, the restoration work of the existing historical structure was undertaken by the architects of Harry Weese & Associates, and the designers of Benjamin Thompson & Associates undertook the job of enhancing the areas not directly under the supervision of the Historic Preservation Review Board. Both firms, in the final analysis, however, interactively solved problems and created the final dynamic spaces that allow the traveler to enjoy the dining and other amenities that once made train travel a glamorous undertaking.

PROJECT NAME:
Hillmann-Garage
LOCATION:
Bremen, Germany
CLIENT:
Steffens KG
ARCHITECT:
von Gerkan, Marg + Partner: Meinhard von
Gerkan, designer; Klaus Staratzke, project
manager; Peter Sembritzki, Klaus Lubbert and
Tuyen Tran Viet, assistants
PHOTOGRAPHY:
Heiner Leska

Hillmann-Garage

Bremen, Germany

A Sculptural Solution

to help alleviate the parking problem in Bremen, Germany von Gerkan, Marg + Partners used reinforced concrete and traditional Northern German brickwork to create the HILLMAN-GARAGE. The lack of adequate parking space in the downtown area necessitated constructing a parking structure in the urban scape. The architects faced the problem of how to design a

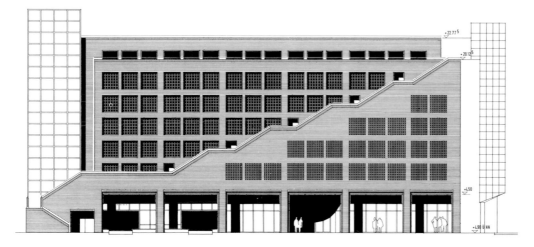

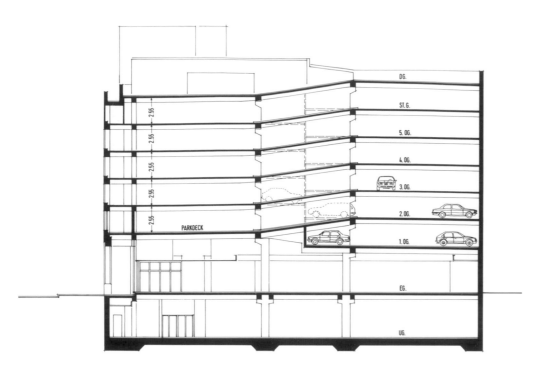

parking structure that would not be purely utilitarian in its expression. One of the design requirements was to build an esthetic link from the new building to the existing structures. They chose to do this with an unusual patterning of brickwork on the facade. The angled and stepped exterior wall expresses the angles and levels of the stairway beyond it, and the square, open brickwork fenestrations allow light and ventilation into the interior.

This building presents a playful and attractive solution to a utilitarian problem and adds a sculptural dimension that brings to mind both the Bauhaus architects and their search for form and function, and the craftsmen of earlier centuries in the articulation and intricate patterns of the brickwork.

The elevator and stair towers are articulated in a glass curtain wall triangular structure which adds interest to the exterior and visually orients the user to different functions of the building.

PROJECT NAME:
Limerick Nuclear Generating Station Unit 2
LOCATION:
Pottstown, Pennsylvania
CLIENT:
Pennsylvania Electric Co.
ARCHITECT:
Bechtel Corp., engineering, procurement, and construction services
PHOTOGRAPHY:
Bechtel Corp.

Limerick Nuclear Generating Station Unit 2

Pottstown, Pennsylvania

The Classic Silhouette

the LIMERICK NUCLEAR GENERATING STATION UNIT 2 in southeastern Pennsylvania designed by the Bechtel Group, Inc. has been given a "1" rating by the Nuclear Regulatory Commission's Systematic Assessment of License Performance (SALP)

Board. "Limerick Unit 2 has proven in every way to be a model project to the industry and a source of pride for all involved in its success." Certainly the image of the towers is the model we all have in our minds of the visual image of nuclear energy.

When one looks at the massive reinforced concrete cooling towers that accompany the nuclear reactor, the image of power and danger are immediately transmitted to our consciousness. The forms are also elegant and beautiful in their own right and are indicative of an energy source that may, in the future, replace our ever-depleting energy sources.

PROJECT NAME:
Susquehanna Steam Electric Station
LOCATION:
NW Of Philadelphia, Pennsylvania, along the
Susquehanna River
CLIENT:
Pennsylvania Power & Light Co.
ARCHITECT:
Bechtel Corp., engineering, procurement,
construction and startup support services
PHOTOGRAPHY:
Bechtel Corp.

Susquehanna Steam
Electric Station

NW of Philadelphia, Pennsylvania
along the Susquehanna River

*Fishing, Hiking, Picnicking
& Nuclear Fission*

t he SUSQUEHANNA STEAM ELECTRIC

STATION, near the town of Berwick,

Pennsylvania is deemed by the Bechtel

Group, Inc., "one of the nuclear power

industry's current success stories." Sited on the banks of the Susquehanna River, this nuclear plant shares the site with a public recreation area that offers fishing, hiking and picnicking.

Again, the silhouettes of the cooling towers are traditional and in the image we expect. The huge concrete structures that house the reactor and the turbine are in the industrial image. One wonders if that's the part that instills fear—the image, the huge masses and the stories of radiation. These plants are a part of our technological environment. When they're built to safety standards, monitored and efficiently-run, they produce a clean form of energy. In fact, this plant had to satisfy several hundred regulatory guides.

PROJECT NAME:
South Texas Nuclear Power Plant
LOCATION:
90 miles SE of Houston, Texas
CLIENT:
Joint owners: Houston Lighting & Power; Central
Power & Light Co. of Corpus Christi; and the cities
of San Antonio, TX and Houston, TX
ARCHITECTS:
Bechtel Corp., engineering, procurement, and
construction management services
PHOTOGRAPHY:
Bechtel Corp.

South Texas Nuclear Power Plant

90 miles SE of Houston, Texas

An Interior View

t his giant blue snake exists in the interior of the turbine building of the SOUTH TEXAS NUCLEAR POWER PLANT 90 miles southeast of Houston, Texas. This plant, also designed by the Bechtel Group, Inc., coexists with a wildlife refuge on an adjacent 7,000 acres. It was designed to be one of the most sophisticated nuclear plants and has three fully-redundant safety systems to shut down the plant in an emergency.

EPILOGUE

Predictions for the Future

"*It is sometimes said of those who try to persuade man of his environmental predicament that they paint a picture so gloomy and irreversible that the average citizen's response is to go out and buy a can of beer. If nothing can be done to escape the onward rush of some irresistible eco-doom, then why take the trouble even to return the can? But indeed over a vast range of environmental problems, action is possible, policies are available, reversals can take place, water run clean, the sun shine over clear cities, the oceans cleanse our human shores, and harvests ripen in uncontaminated fields.*"

Barbara Ward and Rene Dubos—ONLY ONE EARTH
The Care and Maintenance of A Small Planet;
W.W. NORTON & Co., Inc. NEW YORK: 1972

"*One can truly imagine a civilization of tomorrow served and guided by a technology which will no longer be exclusively an arid means to achieve riches for individuals or for certain peoples, or even worse, an inhuman warlike and destroying power, but will mean an intelligent use of the energy and resources of the physical world, and above all, will be the cause and consequence of man's increasingly intimate closeness to the divine wisdom of the creation.*"

"*Even within the realm of the most rigorous technology, the mind remains and will remain completely free to express, interpret and manifest its most profound and mysterious creative forces.*"

Pier Luigi Nervi, "Is Architecture Moving Toward Unchangeable Forms?,"
STRUCTURE IN ART AND IN SCIENCE, Edited by Gyorgy Kepes, GEORGE BRAZILLER, NEW
YORK: 1965

It's become obvious that technology, while it can enhance our lives in marvelous and unexpected ways, asks us to pay a high price when we allow it to control our lives. In order to reduce this price of technology, we are beginning to understand that man must be the master of the machine, not the other way around. Man, the human machine, must become the criteria for what and how we design.

On the preceding pages, this book has shown how architects have used technology in various forms and applications to create structures with more light and space, better ventilating and heating systems and certainly with more sanitary facilities than before the Industrial Revolution. Beyond these practical aspects, this book has shown how architects have used technology to actualize their private visions and their idiosyncratic sense of design. Technology has been used, then, in the service of dreams.

This book has also tried to present alternative building materials—fabric structures, space frames, cable-hung structures, pre-fabricated structures, earth sheltered structures, buildings powered by solar energy, composite structures—and visionary structures. New examples have been illustrated along with historic restorations and retrofits. All the examples illustrated are building forms with a technological component or are building forms that are a direct outgrowth of technology.

SYMBIOSIS & THE CREATIVE PROCESS

However, these design solutions, these completed structures, are not simply a result of technology and the Industrial Revolution. One might say that the raw materials have been shaped, refined and articulated. Creative thinkers have provided us with both innovative design techniques and the materials with which to implement these designs. The inventors gave us new materials. The architects gave us the creative ways in which to use these new materials. In many ways, the inventor and the architect are engaged in a symbiotic relationship.

But, the manufacture of some of the materials, and the implementation of the techniques, has, in many cases, contributed to the pollution of the Planet. This being the case, there are those who propose that the price of technology is too high, the esthetic or practical advantages of these new materials and techniques is too high. Therefore, we should abandon the technological age, return to the craft age—and, thus, save the Planet.

In this thinking, however, there's a major flaw. The Industrial Revolution did not take place by itself. The Industrial Revolution came about as a direct result of the inventions of men—the cotton gin, the converter, the elevator, the steam engine, motion pictures, computerization. Should we destroy all the inventions since the middle of the 19th century and "return to the craft age" of hand-crafted materials for all our daily needs? Would such an experiment truly last?

I'd like to ask another question. By what mechanisms would it be possible to render modern man non-creative, non-inventive, non-visionary? Because that's what it would take to return to the craft age, and *remain* in the craft age.

If you stop and think about it, in order for a society to remain in a non-technological age, you would have to destroy all the existing innovative architecture. To further keep active minds from extrapolating on visual evidence and innovation, you'd also have to burn all the books and paintings that reproduce or describe alternative solutions to design problems. Of course, there would still be those influences in nature that have inspired designers since man first walked the earth—ant hills, sea shells, termite houses, trees, the play of light in different weathers, etc. How would you, or could you, destroy all these inspirations?

THE INHERENT CREATIVE NATURE OF MAN

One of the traits that separates man from the animals is his ability to solve problems in a creative way (animals can think and solve problems, but to a limited extent), and his ability to physically manipulate the environment. This has been happening since man first appeared on the Planet, discovered how to create fire, make the wheel, and so on.

We should also remember that man's "desecration," if you will, of the Planet did not begin with the Industrial Revolution. In point of fact, by the time of the Industrial Revolution, England had consumed almost all of her timber for fuel and had begun mining and burning coal, which also causes pollution. De-foresting causes erosion, floods and a general imbalance in the ecosystem. No age has been free of man's misuse of natural resources,

If we think this through logically, the problem then, is not that man is inventive and constantly creating new technologies with which to build and alter the environment. It's that man does not carefully think through—and plan for—the effects of new technologies on the environment. For the most part (until the present day), man has not believed in the consequences of his actions. Now there is a price to pay, but the price should be reasonable, realistic and should not attempt to push back civilization.

Architects and designers, perhaps more than other professionals, should be aware of how the technologies they employ alter the environment. Because, essentially, that's what they're about—altering the environment. In selecting materials to actualize an idea, the architect, the designer, can favor one material over another if he knows the production of that material is less harmful to the environment. It's an enormous responsibility, but who can make the decisions better than the architect?

EFFICIENT USES OF THE LAND

Zoning is a valuable tool at the disposal of the architect. By using existing zoning laws intelligently and by changing zoning laws that are obsolete, the architect can begin to control the impact of new structures on the environment. Zoning can encompass the uses of land in earthquake zones, flood planes and other areas that could be prone to natural disasters. Nature may be more powerful than man, but man has an advantage in choosing the sites on which he builds.

The architect also has the potential to make creative uses of some zoning regulations. Certainly, the mixed-use buildings we've seen are examples of this; efficient and conservational use of the land can also begin with the client's recommendations and admonitions to the architect. Many clients want to conserve natural areas and provide open spaces as an integral part of a building complex. The architect can also influence the client to begin to think in these terms.

Computer imaging to predict shadow patterns on existing buildings, to model the parking and circulation problems a new structure will bring to a neighborhood—these are tools that can help the architect and the urban landscape. In the past, it was often difficult to predict precisely what the impact of a new structure would be. Now the architect can design within parameters; parameters that help the designer and the inhabitants of any environment.

LEARNING FROM THE PAST

If you study the history of civilization, it becomes obvious that architects and builders in the past were not always aware of what the impact of altering the environment and misusing natural resources might be. The theory is that the inhabitants of Easter Island denuded the forest. Some feel that the cliff dwellers abandoned their civilizations and settlements because of a major drought. Perhaps some phenomena are unavoidable, but certainly deforestation is not. And what of the other so-called ''lost'' civilizations? What drove the inhabitants to abandon sites, villages, cities?

We may never find the answers to these dilemmas, but at least we can plan for our own futures. We can be aware that we do pay a price when we alter the environment. We must be sure the price is worth it—that we have done everything in our power to ensure that each new structure fits into the ecosystem as fully as possible.

THE ARCHITECT/CLIENT PARTNERSHIP

It's not only possible for the architect to educate and influence his client to accept alternative and more efficient energy consumption solutions—as the architect, the designer, the alterer of the landscape, it's his responsibility. In fact, showing the client the alternatives for preserving the natural environment and conserving

energy (to name only two considerations) is in the client's interest both economically and esthetically.

Many of the examples we've shown have incorporated energy-efficient factors into the design process and the final building form. The program for several of the buildings illustrated have charged the architect with maintaining the natural landscape as much as possible. These considerations seem to become more prevalent as awareness of the myriad of plights the environment must face becomes more widespread. These are hopeful signs.

THE FINAL ANALYSIS

Remember these important points when evaluating the role technology plays in the design and altering of our environment:

- Man is intrinsically creative by nature.
- Man has engaged in thoughtless consumption of resources throughout time.
- We must learn from the past and be aware of the reasons why some civilizations have vanished.
- We must make use of land use studies, zoning requirements and computer imaging to model new buildings in the environment.
- The architect is responsible for the education of clients and public concerning the conservation of resources.

None of these points, of course, is a new or revolutionary idea. Most have been discussed and argued pro and con for several generations, but the impact of the past is now irrevocable and the time for debate has past. Now is the time for action.

However, as I previously stated, the signs are hopeful. Earth Day had more publicity and more participation this year than previously. The general public now seems to share the concerns of the design community and the environmentalists. Using technology in responsible ways to improve the lives of the inhabitants of the Planet is an idea whose time has come.

PREDICTIONS FOR THE FUTURE

As a final hopeful note, here are three examples—perhaps futuristic, perhaps simply ultimately sensible—that show how creative thinkers are trying to put technology to use in conserving the resources of our glorious Planet.

WITHOUT ALTERING THE LANDSCAPE

In their design for the 1982 ''Peak'' competition in Hong Kong, THE PEAK, A. & D. Wejchert were concerned that ''any development on the Peak should be confined to the 'natural' idiom to enhance the overall essential balance between man and nature.'' They were concerned with not just adding another manmade geometrical element to the already over built landscape.

To accomplish this feat, the architects would use an in-site reinforced concrete structure. The external wall of the building would be designed as a series of planting boxes arranged in a stepped configuration with windows interspersed. These walls would be constructed of insulated glass reinforced cement units spanning between sloping reinforced concrete columns.

Their design retains the contours of the hilltop by creating a series of "mounds" with open spaces in their centers. From a distance, as the planting grows, the viewer will look up and see the natural form of the hill. The inhabitants of the complex will have all the amenities of conventional housing, but will also have roof gardens with ornamental pools and internal courtyards. Comfortable housing will have been created and the landscape will have been visually preserved, the best of both worlds.

To expand on the both worlds concept, as part of the design program, the buildings presented in this competition had to comply with "Feng-Shui" (the Chinese Art of Placement) concepts. There may be many such ancient design codes and traditions that could help us integrate technology into the natural world.

SOLAR ENERGY AND RECYCLED CONCRETE

"The 'House of the Future' was built to show a wide public that with the aid of technical innovations, living in the immediate future could look utterly different from the way it is now."

These words describe what the designers of *Architectenburo Cees Dam* were trying to accomplish in their HOUSE OF THE FUTURE. This futuristic prototype house not only uses highly developed technologies for solar energy, talking computers, remote control illumination, videophone and a wall composed of living microorganisms; it also is built partly with recycled materials. How much more could one ask of a 21st century house?

All the walls (built from recycled material) are relocatable and the roof of the bathroom opens up like a flower. There are separate toilet seats for men and women, and the toilet is computer controlled. In the door of the toilet compartment is an LCD-screen with satellite television reception. The dish is located outside.

There's a fax machine, teleshopping, telebanking, and word processing. The design is futuristic, spacious and adaptable. It includes a Japanese garden with a teahouse in the pond and works of art; it isn't traditional. It isn't built to resemble a cave and nurture the inhabitants. It's designed and built to make the best use of technology, and of recycling techniques, all desirable attributes in our society.

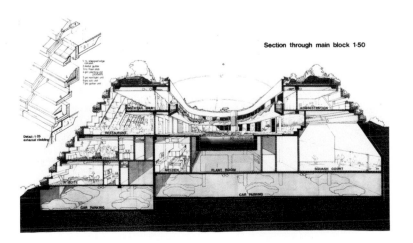

Section through main block 1·50

MORE ELECTRONIC POSSIBILITIES

Our last futuristic example also makes use of highly computerized technologies in the context of an entertainment center, not a residential one. The PYRAMID in Memphis, Tennessee also makes use of the past. It draws on its historical counterpart in Memphis, Egypt for a suitable form for this gigantic structure.

In this structure, instead of giant blocks of stone the architects have used a concrete and steel frame with a cladding of brushed stainless steel interlocking panels. The building will incorporate a basketball arena, a shortwave station, museum facilities and an inclined ride up one corner of the pyramid (in a glass-enclosed car). An observation deck takes up the two top levels.

Inside, in addition to the restaurants and private clubs and tours through the history of American Music, will be the "Memphis to Memphis" experience. For those who have never visited Egypt, this will be the place to see the original Memphis through holographic images. This 321-foot high structure, built in the image of a monument of the past, seeks to bring the past to Tennessee through highly intricate technology. Is this a "Disneyland" experience? The developers hope so.

WHAT TOMORROW MIGHT BRING

If we're lucky, if we carefully evaluate how, why and in what ways we alter our environment, the future could be exciting. More and more, technologies are being developed and presented in theme parks and expositions for our review and study, but we don't have to accept every innovation we see.

Questions have to be asked about each technology. How does it enhance our lives? What are the risks to the environment, either in the production or the implementation? These are not really difficult questions to ask, to ponder, to demand answers to. Yet, they are essential if we are to have a viable lifestyle and a viable planet.

Since the Iron Curtain parted and we've seen the photographs and heard the reports of the extensive damage done by unchecked pollution in Poland, Romania and Czechoslovakia we should take note. There's no point designing innovative structures if there are no people to inhabit them and no plants to enhance them.

INDEX

ARCHITECTS

PROJECTS

PHOTOGRAPHERS